John Ash

**Grammatical Institutes**

Or, an easy introduction to Dr. Lowth's English grammar. Designed for the use of schools, and to lead young gentlemen and ladies, into the knowledge of the first principles of the English language

John Ash

**Grammatical Institutes**
*Or, an easy introduction to Dr. Lowth's English grammar. Designed for the use of schools, and to lead young gentlemen and ladies, into the knowledge of the first principles of the English language*

ISBN/EAN: 9783337248642

Printed in Europe, USA, Canada, Australia, Japan

Cover: Foto ©Paul-Georg Meister /pixelio.de

More available books at **www.hansebooks.com**

OR, AN EASY
# INTRODUCTION
TO

Dr. *Lowth*'s English Grammar,

DESIGNED

FOR THE USE OF SHOOLS,

And to lead Young Gentlemen and Ladies into the Knowledge of the first Principles of the English Language.

By JOHN ASH, LL. D.

WITH AN

APPENDIX,

CONTAINING,

I. The Declension of irregular and defective Verbs.
II. The Application of the Grammatical Institutes.
III. Some Useful Observations on the Ellipsis.
IV. Exercises of Bad English.
V. Lessons on the English Language.

To which are added,

SELECT LESSONS, to instil just Sentiments of Virtue into Youth. And a Collection of Books, proper for Young Gentlemen and Ladies, to shorten the Path to Knowledge.

A NEW EDITION,
Revised and corrected.

---

LONDON;
Printed for CHARLES DILLY, in the Poultry

But then, it has been supposed, even by Men of Learning, that the *English* Tongue is too *vague* and *untractable* to be reduced to any *certain* Standard, or *Rules of Construction*; and that a competent Knowledge of it cannot be attained without an Acquaintance with the *Latin*.

For my Part, I hope these Gentlemen are mistaken, because this would be an invincible Obstacle to the Progress of an *English* Education.

This vulgar Error, for so I beg leave to call it, might perhaps arise from a too partial Fondness for the *Latin;* in which, about two centuries ago, we had the Service of the Church, the Translation of the Bible, and most other Books; few, of any Value.

Value, being then extant in our Mother Tongue.

But now the Case is happily altered. Nor do I think the Error above mentioned would have been so long indulged under the Blessings of the Reformation, had it not been for the many fruitless Attempts which have been made to fix the Grammatical Construction of the *English* Tongue.

Many Gentlemen, who have written on this Subject, have too inconsiderately adopted various Distinctions of the learned Languages, which have no Existence in our own: Many, on the other hand, convinced of this Impropriety, have been too brief, or at least too general, in their Definitions and Rules, running into the quite opposite Extreme: And

And moſt of them, I think, have too much neglected the Peculiarities of the Language on which they wrote.

Theſe Conſiderations have induced me to ſuffer the following little Manual to appear amongſt my Friends, in the Manner it now does. How far it may anſwer the End propoſed, I muſt leave them to determine. If it has any Merit, it muſt be found in Conciſeneſs, Connection, and Application to the proper Genius of our Mother Tongue.

THE first Impression of this little Treatise was attempted some Years ago, purely to oblige a few of the Author's Friends, who were engaged in the Education of Youth: and therefore, at that Time, no Means were made Use of to recommend it to the Public.

Two Editions, however, of this little Book have been since published in London, under the Direction of the Reverend Mr. Ryland, of Northampton, who had, as he says, made full Trial of it in his School, for some Years before, with singular Success.

Thus recommended, it has been well received by the Public; and this Circumstance has induced the Author to revise the original Copy, to which he has now made some Amendments and Additions, which,

*which, he flatters himself, will render it more acceptable and useful to those Gentlemen and Ladies, who may think proper to make Trial of it in their Schools or Families.*

*The Editor of the two Editions above mentioned, was pleased to give this little Manual to the Public, as* The Easiest Introduction to Dr. Lowth's English Grammar; *which Title, in part, it still retains; though the Author is apprehensive it was first printed before the earliest Edition of that valuable Book: and if he has in some few Instances presumed to differ from so great a Man, yet as he has done it on Principles which to him appeared to be satisfactory, he is confident the candid and critical Reader will not impute it to Affectation or Vanity.*

A N

# INTRODUCTION

TO THE

# GRAMMATICAL INSTITUTES.

*Of the* ALPHABET*, *and the* Sounds *of the* Letters.

THE *English Alphabet* consists of *twenty-six* Letters, viz. a, b, c, d, e, f, g, h, i, j, k, l, m, n, o, p, q, r, s, t, u, v, w, x, y, z.

* From *alpha, beta,* the first two *Greek* Letters.

## INTRODUCTION.

Six of thefe Letters, viz. *a, e, i, o, u, y*, are called *Vowels*, from *Vox*, a Voice or Sound, becaufe they make diftinct Sounds of themfelves.

All the Letters in the Alphabet except the Vowels, viz. *b, c, d, f, g, h, j, k, l, m, n, p, q, r, s, t, v, w, x, z*, are called *Confonants*, from *confono*, to found together; becaufe they cannot be founded without fome Vowel joined to them.

*Each* of the *Vowels* has at leaft three *diftinct* Sounds, the *broad* or *full*, the *narrow* or *flender*, and the *middle* or *intermediate*, which will more fully appear from the following Tables.

| Vow. | Broad. | Mid. | | Narrow. |
|------|--------|------|------|---------|
| A.   | all    | an   |      | Ale     |
| E.   | them   | her  |      | me      |
| I.   | bind   | Bird |      | Bill    |
| O.   | Tom    | Ton  | Tone | Tomb    |
| U.   | us     | Ufe  |      | Rule    |
| Y.   | by     | Phyfic |    | Bully   |

# INTRODUCTION.

In the above Sounds we may obferve the following Similarities.

- a. broad  
- o. broad  
} all    Tom

- i. mid.  
- o. mid.  
- u. broad  
} Bird   Ton   us

- e. nar.  
- i. nar.  
- y. nar.  
} me   Bill   Bully

- i. broad  
- y. broad  
} bind   by

- o. nar.  
- u. nar.  
} Tomb   Rule

## A.

*A* is *broad* in moſt Words before *ld, lk, ll*, and *lt;* as *bald, walk, Wall, Altar:* It has likewiſe the *broad* Sound, for the moſt Part, between *w* and *r*, or *t;* as *War, Water.*

B 2        *A* is

*A* is *narrow* in all Words or S[yllables] that are lengthened by the fina[l e;] Babe, Blade, Fate, Relate: It i[s like-] wife *narrow* in all Words comp[ounded] with *ation*; as, Salvation, Rela[tion.]

In moſt other Words the [broad] Sound prevails.

### E.

*E* is for the moſt Part *narrow* [when] it ends a Word; as, Epitome, [Apo-]trophe, me, he, ſhe, be; as likewi[ſe in] Words compounded with *be*; [as, be-]low, beſpeak.

*E* has moſt commonly the [ſame] Sound when it ends a Syllabl[e, if] not joined in Pronunciation to t[he fol-]lowing Conſonants; as, Lever, [elope,] elope, eſcape.

When *E* is joined to the f[ollowing] Conſonants, it is generally pr[onounced] broader; as fell, let, bend.

# INTRODUCTION.

## I.

*I* is always *broad* when the Syllable in which it occurs is made long by the final *e*; as, *Pine, Bite, Lime*: also generally when it goes before *gh, gn, ld, mb*, and *nd*; as, *Sight, Sign, mild, climb, find*.

The *middle* Sound of the *I* is used before *rd*; as, *Bird, third*, and occurs but seldom.

*I* is *narrow* when pronounced *short* with a following Consonant; as, *Pin, Sin, Mill, till*.

## O.

*O* has the *second middle* Sound when the Syllable in which it stands is lengthened by the final *e*: as, *Toe, Doe, Lobe, Robe*. For the other Sounds of this Letter, perhaps no certain Rules can be given.

## U.

The *broad* Sound of the *U* is used, when joined in Pronunciation to the following Consonant; as, *unto, upon, Gun, Pun*.

The *middle* Sound prevails in those Words that are lengthened by the final *e*; as *Mule, mute, refuse, abuse*.

*U* is *narrow* when it comes after *r*, and is pronounced long, or not immediately joined to the following Consonant; as, *rude, Ruby, Ruin*.

## Y.

*Y*, at the end of a Word of one Syllable, or such as are accented on the last Syllable, is *broad*; as, *Sky, fly, try, comply*: But in the End of Words of more than one Syllable, and not accented on the last, it is generally *narrow*; as, *possibly, Folly, Poverty*.

*All Vowels*, when pronounced *short* and negligently with a following Consonant,

sonant, in a Syllable not accented, have nearly the same Sound; as, *Altar*, *alter*, *Manor*, *Murmur*, *Satyr*.

## Of DIPHTHONGS*.

WHEN two Vowels meet in the same Syllable, they make what is called a *Diphthong*.

Threre are no less than twenty *Diphthongs* in the English Language; which with their Sounds are expressed in the following Tables.

| Diph. | Broad | Middle | Narr. S. |
|---|---|---|---|
| aa. | Balaam | Isaac | |
| ai. | Praise | | |
| au. | Author | Aunt | Gauge |
| aw. | Awl | | |
| ay. | say | | |
| ea. | Beam | Bread | Heart |
| ee. | see | | |
| ei. | Vein | | eight |
| eo. | George | Leopard | People |
| eu. | | | Feud |
| ew. | | | few |
| ey. | Eye | | Key |

* From *dis*, twice, *Phthorgos*, a Sound.

*Diph.*

| Diph. | Broad | Middle | Narr. S. |
|---|---|---|---|
| ie. | Cashier | Friend | Chief |
| oa. | Boat | | |
| oi. | Oil | — | |
| oo. | Floor | Flood | Food |
| ou. | Soul | Couple | could |
| ow. | mow | now | |
| oy. | convoy | | |
| ui. | Guide | build | Fruit |

To these we may add *ae* and *oe*, which are used only in Words derived from the *Latin* and *Greek*; as, *Cæsar*, *Phœbe*; and chiefly retained in proper Names.

When three Vowels meet together in a Syllable, they make a *Triphthong*; as,

| | | | |
|---|---|---|---|
| eau. | Beauty | uai. | quaint |
| eye. | Eye | uea. | queasy |
| ieu. | Lieu | uee. | queer |
| iew. | View | you. | young |

Unless *y* at the Beginning of Syllables be a Consonant, which some Authors will not allow it to be, in any Case whatsoever.

Here we may observe, that though the Vowels and Diphthongs, and the Words in which their different Sounds occur,

occur, are so numerous, yet, perhaps, there are not many more than a Dozen full and distinct Vowel Sounds in the English Language; which, I think, will appear to any one who carefully consults the foregoing Tables.

## *Of* CONSONANTS.

### C.

*C* has two Modifications, the *hard*, and the *soft;* as, *cull, Cell.*

*C* is always *hard*, like *K*, before *a, o, u*, and *all Consonants*, and at the *End* of Syllables or Words, as. *call, Coal, cut, accost, public.* But *soft*, like *S*, before *e, i,* and *y;* as, *cease, Cit, cypress.*

### G.

*G* has likewise a *hard* and a *soft* Modification; as, *Gun, Gin.*

*G* is *hard* before *a, o, u,* and *all Consonants*, and at the *End* of Words; as, *gat, got, Gut, glad, Jug.*

*G* is

*G* is for the most Part *soft* before *e*, *i*, and *y*; as, *Gem, Gill, Clergy*: But all proper Names in the Bible have *G* hard before *e* and *i*; as *Gera, Gilboah.* *G* is likewise hard in many English Words before *e* and *i*: as, *Geese, geld, get, Gear, Girl, give, giddy, Dagger, Anger:* And in many more which may be supplied by Observation.

### Ch.

*Ch* has one *hard*, and two *soft* Modifications; as, *Baruch* (Baruk), *Arch, Chaise* (Shaise). The *first* prevails in Words of *Hebrew* and *Greek* Original, and the *last* in such as, come from the *French*.

### Ph.

*Ph*, when joined in the same Syllable, is sounded like *F*; as, *Asaph, Elephant.*

### S.

*S* has two Modifications, a *sharp* and a *flat*; as, *this, these.* The *flat* Sound prevails in the End of all Words made plural.

# INTRODUCTION.  xix

plural, or otherwise increased by the Addition of *s*; as, *Pins, Foxes, loves.*

### Th.

*Th* has likewise a *sharp* and a *flat* Sound; as, *thin, thine.*

### Ti.

*Ti* before a Vowel is frequently softened down to *sh'*; as, *Station*, in which the Sound of the *i* is nearly, if not quite, lost.

### W.

*W* in Diphthongs and Triphthongs, as in *few, View*, must be a Vowel: But in other Cases, especially in the Beginning of Words, it must be a *Consonant*; as, *We, William.*

## *Of the* POINTS *or* STOPS, *and other Characters made Use of in Writing.*

A *Comma* [,] denoting perhaps, especially in long Sentences, a *little* Elevation of the Voice, is the *shortest*

## INTRODUCTION.

*shortest* Pause, and may be held while you count *one*.

A *Semicolon* [ ; ] denoting for the most Part an *Evenness* of the Voice, may be held while you count *two*.

A *Colon* [ : ] marks a *little* Depression of the Voice, and requires a Pause while you count *three*.

A *Period* [ . ] is a *full Stop*, denoting a yet *greater* Depression of the Voice than a Colon, and may be held while you count *four*.

A *Note* of *Interrogation* [ ? ] is placed at the End of a *Question*, and denotes an Elevation of the Voice, and rather a Smartness in the Pronunciation.

A *Note of Admiration* [ ! ] is used after a Word or Sentence that expresses Surprise or Emotion, and denotes a Modulation of the Voice suited to the Expression.

## INTRODUCTION.

A *Quotation* ['—' or "—"] includes a Sentence, &c. taken from an Author, or introduced as spoken by another.

A *Parenthesis (to be avoided as much as possible)* is used to include one Sentence in another, and denotes a Suppression of the Voice and a hasty Pronunciation.

A *Caret* [∧] denotes an Interlineation, and shews where to bring in what was omitted in the first writing.

A *Hyphen* [-] is used to join the Parts of a Word together, especially such as are written partly in one Line and partly in another. The Word in this Case is to be divided according to the most natural and approved Rules for the Division of Syllables.

An *Apostrophe* ['] is a Sign of Contraction; as, *lov'd*, for *loved*.

A *Paragraph* [¶] is sometimes used to distinguish the Beginning of a new Subject.

A *Diæresis*

## INTRODUCTION.

A *Diæresis* [ ·· ] is used to divide two Vowels which would otherwise be sounded together.

Several Notes, as, an *Asterisk* [*], an *Obelisk*, &c. [ †, ‡, ‖ ] are used as References to some Observations in the Margin.

The Learner may observe that the *following Words* are *always distinguished* in Writing by a capital Letter, viz.

The *first* Word of any *Writing, Letter*, or *Discourse*: the *next* Word after a *Period*: The *Pronoun I*, and the *Interjection O*: The *first* Word of every Sentence *taken from an Author, or introduced as spoken by another:* Every *Title* and *proper Name* of a Place or Person: And the *first* Word of every *Line* or *Verse* in *Poetry*.

Many *Authors* of the first Rank choose to begin every *Noun* or *Substantive* with a *Capital; some*, the *next* Word after a *Colon*: and *others, remarkable Adjectives*, and such as are put *absolutely.*

*Grammatical* INSTITUTES:

OR,

GRAMMAR*,

Adapted  English Tongue.

1. IN *English* there are *ten* Kinds of Words or Parts of Speech, *viz.*

*Article, Noun, Adjective, Pronoun, Verb, Participle, Adverb, Conjunction, Preposition,* and *Interjection.*

* From the *Greek* Word *Gramma*, a Letter: And is the Art of expressing our Thoughts with Propriety, either in Speaking or Writing.

## Of an ARTICLE*.

2. AN *Article* is a Part of Speech set before *Nouns* to fix their vague Signification: as, *a* Man, *the* Man; *an* House, *the* House. The Articles are, *an, a,* and *the.*

## Of a NOUN†.

3. A *Noun*, or *Substantive* is the Name of a *Person, Place,* or *Thing;* as, *John, London,* Honor, Goodness.

4. There are *two Numbers:* The *Singular*, which speaks of *one;* as a Man, a Troop: and the *Plural*, which speaks of *more than one;* as, Men, Troops.

5. The *Plural* is usually formed by adding *s* to the *Singular*: as, Noun, Nouns; Verb, Verbs,

---

* From the *Latin* Word *Articulus*, a Joint or small Part.

† From *Nomen*, a Name.

6. When

# INSTITUTES.

6. When the *Singular* ends in *s*, *x*, *ch*, or *sh*, the *Plural* is formed by adding the Syllable *es;* as, Miss, *Misses;* Box, *Boxes;* Peach, *Peaches;* Brush, *Brushes.*

7. When the *Singular* ends in *y* with a *Consonant* before it, the *Plural* is formed by changing the *y* into *ies:* as, Lady, *Ladies;* Cherry, *Cherries.* When the *Singular* ends in *f*, or *fe*, the *Plural* is formed by changing the *f* or *fe* into *ves:* as, Life, *Lives;* Half, *Halves,* &c. except *Dwarf, Grief, Hoof, Muff,* &c. which take *s,* to make the *Plural.*

8. Sometimes the *Plural* is formed by adding the Syllable *en;* as, Ox, *Oxen:* sometimes by *changing* the *Vowel;* as, Man, *Men:* and sometimes by changing the *Vowels* and *Consonants;* as, Penny, *Pence;* Mouse, *Mice.*

9. Some few Words coming immediately from the *Hebrew,* form the *Plural* by adding *im* to the *Singular:* as, Cherub, *Cherubim;* Seraph, *Seraphim.* Some from the *Greek,* ending in *on,* change the *on* into *a;* as, Phænomenon,

nomenon, *Phænomena.* Some from the *Latin* in *us,* change the *us* into *i*: as, Radius, *Radii;* Magus, *Magi.*

10. Some Nouns have *no Plural;* as, *Wheat,* &c. others *no Singular;* as, *Ashes,* &c: and some are the *same* in *both* Numbers; as, *Sheep,* &c.

11. There are *two Genders* \*; the *Masculine* †, and the *Feminine* ‡.

12. The *Masculine* denotes the *He-kind;* as, a. *Man,* a *Prince.*

13. The *Feminine* denotes the *She-kind;* as, a *Woman,* a *Princess.*

14. Nouns signifying Things *without Life,* are *properly* of *no Gender;* as, a *Pen,* a *Table.*

15. By a common Figure in the *English Tongue,* the *Sun* is of the *Masculine;* the *Moon,* the *Church,* Ships,

---

\* From *Genus,* a Sex or Kind.
† From *Mas,* the Male-kind.
‡ From *Femina,* a Woman.

and

and frequently *Countries* and *Virtues*, such as *France, Spain, Faith, Hope,* &c. are of the *feminine Gender*.

16. Here likewise it may be necessary to observe,

| *Masculine.* | *Feminine.* |
|---|---|
| Abbot | Abbess |
| Actor | Actress |
| Adulterer | Adulteress |
| Ambassador | Ambassadress |
| Administrator | Administratrix |
| Baron | Baroness |
| Bachelor | Maid |
| Boar | Sow |
| Boy | Girl |
| Bridegroom | Bride |
| Brother | Sister |
| Buck | Doe |
| Bull | Cow |
| Bullock | Heifer |
| Cock | Hen |
| Count | Countess |
| Duke | Dutchess |
| Dog | Bitch |
| Deacon | Deaconess |
| Drake | Duck |

Elector

|   *Masc.*   |   *Fem.*     |
|-------------|--------------|
| Elector     | Electress    |
| Executor    | Executrix    |
| Emperor     | Empress      |
| Father      | Mother       |
| Friar       | Nun          |
| Governor    | Governess    |
| Gander      | Goose        |
| Husband     | Wife         |
| Horse       | Mare         |
| Heir        | Heiress      |
| Hunter      | Huntress     |
| Jew         | Jewess       |
| King        | Queen        |
| Lord        | Lady         |
| Lad         | Lass         |
| Lion        | Lioness      |
| Marquis     | Marchioness  |
| Man         | Woman        |
| Master      | Mistress     |
| Milter      | Spawner      |
| Nephew      | Niece        |
| Prince      | Princess     |
| Prophet     | Prophetess   |
| Poet        | Poetess      |
| Patron      | Patroness    |
| Ram         | Ewe          |
| Son         | Daughter     |

# INSTITUTES. 29

| *Masc.* | *Fem.* |
|---|---|
| Stag | Hind |
| Shepherd | Shepherdess |
| Tutor | Tutoress |
| Viscount | Viscountess |
| Uncle | Aunt |
| Widower | Widow |
| Wizard | Witch |
| Whoremonger | Whore. |

17. *Nouns* have *two Cases* ; the *Nominative\**, and the *Genitive* †. The *genitive* Case is formed by adding *s*, with an *Apostrophe* to the *Nominative* : as, Men, *Men's* ; Ox, *Ox's*.

\* From *nominativus (a nomino)*, naming.
† From *genitivus (a gigno)*, natural or belonging to, and therefore some Authors have called it the *possessive* Case.

NOTE 17. In the Formation of this Case, I have complied with a late Refinement, and what I really think a corrupt Custom. The *genitive* Case in my Opinion, might be much more properly formed by adding *s*, or, when the Pronunciation requires it, *es* without an *apostrophe* ; as, Men, *Mens* ; Ox, *Oxes* ; Horse, *ses* ; Ass, *Asses*.

This

This Case undoubtedly came from the *Saxon*; and the best *English* Writers after the *Norman* Conquest, even down to the Time of *Chaucer* and the Reformation, formed it just in the same Manner they did the *plural* Number, viz. by the Addition of *s, es,* or *is*; and were rather sparing in the Use of it. After that the *is* and *es* were discontinued by Degrees, though the latter, in a few Instances, is retained to this Day in the Version of the Bible.

As to the *Apostrophe*, it was seldom used to distinguish the *genitive* Case till about the Beginning of the present Century, and then seems to have been introduced by Mistake. At that Time the *genitive* Case was supposed to have had its Original from a Contraction; as, *John's Book*, for *John his Book*: But that Notion has been sufficiently exploded: And therefore the Use of the Apostrophe, especially in those Instances where the Pronunciation requires an additional Syllable, is, I presume, quite indefensible. To write *Ox's, Ass's, Fox's,* and at the same Time pronounce it *Oxes, Asses, Foxes,* is such a Departure from the original Formation, at least in Writing, and such an inconsistent Use of the *Apostrophe*, as cannot be equalled perhaps in any other Language; and though it may be said that the *Apostrophe* has some Propriety as a Note of Distinction, yet no one, I think, who has any Knowledge of Grammar, can well mistake the *plural* Number for the *genitive* Case. However, it appears to me, at present, to be a Distinction of v little Importance. Formerly there were Notes used to distinguish the *ablative Case singular* of *Latin* Nouns of the first *Declension*, and the *genitive* of the fourth, which are now laid aside by correct Writers; and I cannot but think that, some Time or other, this will be the Fate of the *Apostrophe* in the *genitive* Case.

## *Of an* ADJECTIVE*.

18. AN *Adjective* is a Word that signifies the *Quality* of any Person, Place, or Thing; as, a *good* Man, a *great* City, a *fine* House.

19. Most *Adjectives* have, at least, two Degrees of *Comparison*; which are commonly called the *Comparative* and the *Superlative*.

20. The *Comparative* is formed, for the most part, by adding *er* to the *Positive*; as, long, *longer;* short, *shorter;*

* From *ad*, to, and *jacio*, to put.

NOTE 20. *Long* is the *positive* State of the *Adjective:* and therefore, as many Authors observe, cannot be *properly* called a *Step* or *Degree*.

The

The *Superlative*, by adding *est*; as, long, *longest*, &c.

21. These *Degrees* of *Comparison* are frequently formed by the *Adverbs*, *very*, *infinitely*, *more*, *most*, *less*, *least*: as *more* short, *very*, *most*, or *infinitely* short; *less* common, *least* common, *&c.*

22. There are a *few* Adjectives peculiar in their Comparison; as, *good*, *better*, *best*; *bad*, *worse*, *worst*, &c.

## Of a PRONOUN*.

23. A *Pronoun* is a Word used *instead* of a Noun, to avoid the too frequent Repetition of the *same* Word; as, "The Man is merry, *he* laughs, *he* sings."

24. The following *Pronouns* (*it* only excepted) have *three Cases, Nominative*,

---

* From *pro*, for, and *Nomen*, a Noun.

Geni...

# INSTITUTES.

*Genitive* and *Accusative* * in each number.

Singular.

| Sing. | Plu. |
|---|---|
| *Nom.* I | We |
| *Gen.* mine, my | ours |
| *Acc.* me | us |
| *Nom.* Thou | Ye, you |
| *Gen.* thine, thy | your's your |
| *Acc.* thee | you |

| *Nom.* | *Gen.* | *Acc.* |
|---|---|---|
| He | his | him |
| She | hers, her | her |
| It | its | |

* From *causo*, to accuse, because this Case receives the Force or Accusation of the Verb.

NOTE 24. Some Grammarians would have *mine, thine, ours, yours*, &c. to be the only genitive Cases, of the primitive Pronouns; and *my, thy*, &c. to be pronominal Adjectives derived from them: but as *his* and *its*, which are confessedly genitive Cases, are joined to Nouns, as well as *my, thy*, &c. I thought best to range them as I have done above, and shall provide for the proper Use of each Variation in the Rules of Syntax.

D                    Plural.

*Plural.*

| Nom. | Gen. | Acc. |
|---|---|---|
| They | theirs, their | them |

25. *Who, whosoever,* and the Pronominal Adjectives, *one, other,* and *another,* are thus varied.

*Singular and Plural.*

| Nom. | Gen. | Acc. |
|---|---|---|
| Who | whose | whom |
| whosoever | whosesoever | whomsoever |

*Sing.*        *Plu.*

| Nom. | Gen. | |
|---|---|---|
| One | ones | ones |
| other | others | |
| another | anothers | other, others |

26. The following have,

| *Sing.* | *Plu.* |
|---|---|
| This | these |
| that | those |
| myself, oneself, ourself | ourselves |
| thyself, yourself | yourselves |
| himself, herself, itself | themselves |

27. Those

# INSTITUTES. 35

27. Those that follow are *further* distinguished by their *Genders*.

| *Masc.* | *Fem.* | *No Gender.* |
|---|---|---|
| He | she | it |
| his | hers | its |
| him | her | |
| himself | herself | itself |

28. *Pronominal* Adjectives, such as *ten, forty, fifty,* &c. and some others, seem to have a *genitive* Case regularly formed by adding *s* to the *Nominative;* as, ten, *tens.*

NOTE. The other Pronouns, *which, what,* &c. have no *Variation.*

## *Of a* VERB*.

29. A *Verb* is a Word that signifies the *Acting* or *Being* of a Person, Place, or Thing; as, the Man *calls,* the City *stands,* the Tree *falls,* I *am.*

* From *Verbum*, a Word. A Verb being the principal Word in a Sentence.

D 2              30. The

30. The Verb that signifies *merely Being* is *neuter*; as, I *am*, he *is:* Verbs that signify *doing* are *active*; as, I *speak* the Word, I *wrote* the Letter.

31. The

NOTE 30. Properly speaking, there is *no passive* Verb in the *English* Language; for though I *am loved*, is commonly called a *passive* Verb yet *loved* is no Part of the *Verb*, but a *Participle*, or *Adjective*, derived of the Verb *love*.

I am very sensible that the greatest Man * perhaps, that ever yet wrote on this Subject, is of a different Opinion. He says. "There are "three Kinds of Verbs; *active, passive*, and "*neuter*." And when he comes to the grammatical Resolution of this Sentence, "In "whom I *am* well *pleased*," he tells us—— "That *am* is the indicative Mode, present "Time, and first Person singular of the neuter "Verb, *to be; well*, an Adverb; *pleased*, the "passive Participle of the Verb *to please*, making with the auxiliary Verb am, a *passive Verb*." The Consideration of this, I must confess, could by no Means induce me to suppress the above Note.

In Parsing, every Word should be considered as a distinct Part of Speech: For though two or more Words may be united to form a Mode, a Tense, or a Comparison; yet

* Dr. *Lowth*, followed by *Buchanan*.

31. The *Noun* or *Pronoun* that stands *before* the *active* Verbs in the above Examples, may be called the *Agent*, and that which stands *before* the *neuter*, the *Subject* of the Verb; But the *Noun* or *Pronoun* that *follows* the *active* Verbs, in the same Examples, may be called the *Object* of the Verb.

32. There are *four Modes* \*, or Ways of using the Verb; the *Indicative*, the *Imperative*, the *Potential*, and the *Infinitive*.

33. The *Indicative* † expresses the Action or Being, *directly* and *absolutely*; as, I *am*, he *loves*.

it seems quite improper to unite two or more Words to make a Noun, a Verb, an Adjective, &c.

Verbs *intransitive*, or such as do not pass over or convey their Force to any Object, as *sleep, walk, run*, &c. are commonly, though perhaps not very properly, called *neuter* Verbs.

\* From *Modus*, a Manner.
† From *indico*, to shew.

34. The *Imperative* \* commands or forbids; as, *come, go, fear* him, *love* him.

35. The *Potential* † expresses the Action or Being, as *possible* or *impossible, fit* or *unfit*; as, I *may love,* I *may not love.*

36. The *Infinitive* ‡ expresses the Action or Being, *indeterminately*; as, *to be, to love.*

---

\* From *impero*, to command.
† From *potentialis (a possum)*, to be able.
‡ From *infinitivus*, without Bounds.

Note 35. This Mode or Form of the Verb does not, I think, in any Case coincide with the *Indicative*. It always has some Respect to the *Power, Will,* &c. of the Agent, by which, even when Conditionality is out of the Question, it is distinguished from the merely declarative Form: The one declares the Action done, or to be done, without any further Consideration: the other declares not the Action done, or to be done, but the *Ability, Inability,* &c. of the Agent to perform that Action; and is therefore properly stiled the *potential* Mode.

37. There

## INSTITUTES.

37. There are *five Tenses*, or *Times;* the *Present*, the *Imperfect*, the *Perfect*, the *Pluperfect*, and the *Future*.

38. The *Present* expresses the Time that *now is:* as, I *love;* or, *am loving*.

39. The *Imperfect* denotes the Time *past indeterminately:* as, I *loved;* or, *was loving*.

40. The *Perfect* denotes the Time *past determinately:* as, I *have loved;* or, *have been loving*.

41. The *Pluperfect* denotes the Time *past*, as prior to some other Point of Time specified in the Sentence: as, I *had loved;* or, *had been loving*.

42. The *Future* denotes the Time *to come:* as, I *will* or *shall love;* or, *will* or *shall be loving*.

43. These

---

NOTE 42. These Formations of the several Tenses seem to have Respect *both* to the *Time* and *State* of the Action signified by the Verb.

43. These *Modes* and *Tenses* are partly formed by the *Verb itself*, and partly by the Assistance of *Signs*.

The *present* Tense denotes the *Time* that *now is*, and the Action *unfinished*: as, I *write*, or I *am now writing* the Letter. The *Imperfect* denotes the *Time past indeterminately*, and the Action *to have been completed* at any past Time that may be specified: as, I *wrote* the Letter, or I *began* and *finished the Writing* of the Letter, this Morning, Yesterday, a Week ago, &c. The *Perfect* denotes the *Time just past*, and the *Action fully completed*: as, I *have written* the Letter, or I *have just now finished the Writing* of the Letter. The *Pluperfect* denotes the *Time past* and the Action *to have been completed prior* to some other Circumstance specified in the Sentence: as, I *had written* the Letter, or I *had finished the Writing* of the Letter, before you came in. The *Future* denotes the *Time to come*, and the Action *to be completed* at any future Time that may be mentioned: as, I *will write* the Letter, or I *will begin* and *finish the Writing* of the Letter, to-night, to morrow, &c.

The *other* Forms of these Tenses, viz. I *am writing*, I *was writing*, I *have been writing*, I *had been writing*, I *will be writing*, seem for the most Part to leave the Action *undetermined*.

44. There

44. There are *two Modes* formed from the *Verb itself:* The *Indicative;* as, I *love:* and the *Imperative;* as, *love* thou. And likewise *two Tenses;* the *present;* as, I *love:* and the *Past;* as, I *loved.*

45. The *auxiliary* \* *Signs* are *to, do, did, have, had, shall, will, may, can, must, might, would, could, should.*

46. *To,* is a Sign of the *infinitive Mode:* as, *to* be; *to* love.

47. *May, can, must, might, would, could, should,* and their Inflections †, *mayst, canst, mightest, wouldest, couldest, shouldest,* are Signs of the *potential* Mode.

48. *Do,* and its Inflections, *dost, doth,* or *does,* are Signs of the *present* Tense.

49. *Did,* and its Inflection, *didst,* are Signs of the *imperfect* Tense.

\* From *auxilior,* to help.
† From *inflecto,* to change (the Ending).

50. *Have,*

50. *Have*, and its Inflections, *haſt*, *hath*, or *has*, are Signs of the *perfect* Tenſe.

51. *Had*, and its Inflection, *hadſt*, are Signs of the *pluperfect* Tenſe.

52. *Shall* and *will*, and their Inflections, *ſhalt* and *wilt*, are Signs of the *future* Tenſe.

53. In Verbs there is a Reference to *three Perſons* in each Number: as, *Singular*, I *love*, thou *loveſt*, he *loveth*; *Plural*, We *love*, ye *love*, they *love*.

The *ſecond* Perſon of the Verb in the *ſingular* Number is formed out of the *firſt*, by adding *eſt*, or *ſt*; the *third*, by adding *eth*, *th*, *es*, or only *s*.

NOTE. The auxiliary Signs ſeem to have the Nature of Adverbs.

*Do*, *have*, and *will*, when they are not join'd to Verbs to *diſtinguiſh* the *Circumſtance* of *Time*, are abſolutely Verbs: as, I *do* it, I *have* it, I *will* it.

# INSTITUTES. 43

*St* is added instead of *est*; *th*, instead of *eth*, to Verbs ending in *e*: as, love, lov*est*; prove, prov*eth*: *es* to such as end in *ss*, *x*, and *o*: as, pass, pass*es*; fix, fix*es*; go, go*es*. When *est* or *eth* is added to a Verb ending in a *single Consonant*, preceded by a *single Vowel* bearing the Accent, that *Consonant* is doubled; as, *forget, forgettest, forgetteth*.

54. The *first* Person *speaks of himself*; as, "*I John* take thee Elizabeth."

55. The *second* Person has the Speech directed *to him*, and is supposed to be *present*; as, "*Thou Harry* art a wicked "Fellow."

56. The *third* Person is *spoken of*, or described, and supposed to be *absent*; as, "*That Thomas* is a good Man."

57. The *Verb itself* has but *two Terminations respecting Time*: as, *love*, and *loved*; which last may be called the Inflection of the *preter* or *past Tense*: And when this Inflection of the *preter* Tense is formed by adding *d,* or *ed,*
to

to the *first Person Present Tense*, the Verb is *regular*, and is declined after the following Examples.

### INDICATIVE MODE.
#### *Present Tense.*

58. *Sing.* I love or do love, thou lovest or dost love, he loveth or loves, or doth or does love. *Plu.* We love or do love, ye or you love or do love, they love or do love.

#### *Imperfect Tense.*

59. *Sing.* I loved or did love, thou lovedst or didst love, he loved or did love. *Plu.* We loved or did love, ye loved or did love, they loved or did love.

#### *Perfect Tense.*

60. *Sing.* I have loved, thou hast loved, he hath loved. *Plu.* We have loved, ye have loved, they have loved.

#### *Pluperfect Tense.*

61. *Sing.* I had loved, thou hadst loved, he had loved. *Plu.* We had loved, ye had loved, they had loved.

*Futur*

*Future Tense.*

62. *Sing.* I shall or will love, thou shalt or wilt love, he shall or will love. *Plu.* We shall or will love, ye shall or will love, they shall or will love.

63. *Some Verbs* in this Mode will admit of a *second Future*, especially such as signify the *completing* of any Thing; as, I *shall or will have finished* it to-morrow.

IMPERATIVE MODE.

64. *Sing.* Love, do thou love, or love thou. *Plu.* Love, do ye love, or love ye.

NOTE 64. *Let*, commonly called a *Sign* of the the Imperative Mode, is *properly a Verb* in that Mode; as in the Example, *let him love*, the Meaning is, *permit* or *suffer* him to *love*: *Let*, therefore, seems to be a Verb of the *imperativ*, and *love* of the *infinitive* Mode; the Sign, *to*, being understood, though not expressed.

E POTEN-

*Present Tense.*

65. *Sing.* I muſt, may, can, would, could, or ſhould love; thou muſt, mayeſt, canſt, wouldeſt, couldeſt, or ſhouldeſt love; he muſt, may, can, would, could, or ſhould love. *Plu.* We muſt, may, can, would, could, or ſhould love; ye, &c.

*Perfect Tense.*

66. *Sing.* I muſt, might, would, could, or ſhould have loved; thou muſt, mighteſt, wouldeſt, couldeſt, or ſhouldeſt have loved; he muſt, might, would, could, or ſhould have loved. *Plu.* We muſt, might, would, could, or ſhould have loved; ye, &c.

67. The *pluperfect* Tenſe, in *this Mode,* is *beſt* expreſſed by the *perfect:* as, I *might have* loved her before the Time you mention.

68. The *future Tenſe* of *moſt Verbs,* in *this Mode,* is *beſt* expreſſed by the *preſent:* as, I *may love* to-morrow.

69. There

69. There is a *subjunctive** or *conditional* Form, which *drops* the *personal Terminations* in certain Tenses of this Mode; as, though thou *love*, though he *love*.

## INFINITIVE MODE.

70. *Present Tense*, to love; *Perfect*, to have loved; *Future*, about to love.

## THE DECLENSION OF THE NEUTER VERB.

### INDICATIVE MODE.

*Present Tense.*

71. *Sing.* I am, thou art, he is. *Plu.* We are, ye or you are, they are.

*Imperfect Tense.*

72. *Sing.* I was, thou wast, he was. *Plu.* We were, ye were, they were.

---

* From *sub*, under, and *jungo*, to join.

*Perfect Tense.*

73. *Sing.* I have been, thou haſt been, he hath, or has been. *Plu.* We have been, ye have been, they have been.

*Pluperfect Tense.*

74. *Sing.* I had been, thou hadſt been, he had been. *Plu.* We had been, ye had been, they had been.

*Future Tense.*

75. *Sing.* I ſhall or will be, thou ſhalt or wilt be, he ſhall or will be.— *Plu.* We ſhall or will be, ye ſhall or will be, &c.

*Second Future.*

76. *Sing.* I ſhall or will have been, &c.

IMPERATIVE MODE.

78. *Sing.* Be, do thou be, or be thou. *Plu.* Be, do ye be, or be ye.

POTEN-

# POTENTIAL MODE.

*Present Tense.*

79. *Sing.* I muſt, may, can, would, could, or ſhould be; thou muſt, mayeſt, canſt, wouldeſt, couldeſt, or ſhouldeſt be; he, &c. *Plu.* We muſt, may, can, would, could, or ſhould be, ye, &c.

*Perfect and pluperfect Tenses.*

80. *Sing.* I muſt might, would, could, or ſhould have been; thou muſt, mighteſt, wouldeſt, couldeſt, or ſhouldeſt have been; he muſt, might, would, could, or ſhould have been. *Plu.* We muſt, might, would, could, or ſhould have been; ye, &c.

81. The *future Tense*, in *this Mode*, is *beſt* expereſſed by the *preſent:* as, I *may be* to-morrow.

82. The *ſubjunctive* Form of this Verb is thus diſtinguiſhed:

*Present Tense.*

*Sing.* Though I be, though thou be, though he be. *Plu.* Though we be, though ye be, though they be.

*Imperfect Tense.*

*Sing.* Though I were, though thou wert, though he were. *Plu.* Though we were, though ye were, though they were.

INFINITIVE MODE.

83 *Present,* to be; *Perfect* to have been; *Future,* about to be.

84. When the *Termination* of the *preter* Tense is not formed by adding *d,* or *ed,* to the *first Person of* the *present* Tense *singular,* the Verb may be called *irregular;* but that *Irregularity* being discovered and observed in the *preter* Tenses, the Verb is declined, in *all other Respects,* as the *regular* Verb.

85. The moſt *common Irregularity* is when the *d*, or *ed*, for better Sound's Sake, is changed into *t;* and this is, for the moſt Part, the Caſe, when the Verb itſelf ends in *f, p*, and *x*: as, *puft, wrapt*, and *mixt*; for *puffed, wrapped,* and *mixed*, &c.

NOTE. The *ſame Irregularity*, or Contraction frequently occurs in Verbs of other *Terminations*. For ſome *different Irregularities* we refer to the following Head of *Participles*.

## *Of a* PARTICIPLE*.

86. A *Participle* is *derived* of a *Verb,* and *partakes* of the Nature both of the *Verb* and the *Adjective*.

87. There

From *participio*, to partake.

* NOTE 86. The *Participle*, ſo far as it expreſſes the *Circumſtance* of the Noun to which it is joined by the neuter Verb, has the *Nature* of an *Adjective:* but, as implying the *Action* of ſome *Agent*, it has the *Nature* of the *Verb*.

87. There are *two Participles*, pertaining to the Verbs; the *active*, which
always

The *Passive* Participle seems to have been invented more fully to express that *Influence* or *Dependence* which the *Agent* and *Object* of a Verb have on each other: as, " *John* loves *Elizabeth;* " or, *Elizabeth* is loved by *John.* The *King* " wrote the *Letter;* or, the *Letter* was *written* " by *the King.*"

Here *loved* and *written*, so far as they express the *Circumstances* of the Nouns to which they are joined by the neuter Verb, *may be considered as Adjectives;* but in another View, as they imply the *Action* or *Force* of some *Agent* or *compulsive* Cause, *they may be considered as Verbs.*

Hence it is, that *Verbs intransitive*, which have no Object, can have no *passive* Participle; some of them have a *participial* Form joined to the neuter Verb: as, " The Man is *fallen;* The Sun is *risen.*" But as *fallen* and *risen* have no Reference to any Agent or compulsive Cause different from the Subject of the Verb, so they cannot with any Propriety be denominated *passive* Participles: And, notwithstanding their Form, they differ very little, if any Thing, from common Adjectives.

The

*always* ends in *ing*; and the *passive* which for the *most* Part ends in *ed*; as, from the Verb *call* are derived the Participles *calling* and *called*. In the Formation of the Participles, if the Verb ends in *e*, the *e* is omitted; as, love, *loving, loved*. If it ends in a *single Consonant*, preceded by a *single Vowel* bearing the Accent, that *Consonant* is *doubled*; as, commit, *committing, committed*.

The same Thing may be observed of the *active* Participle; as, " The Master is *writing*, the Horse is *trotting*." Here the Participle implies both the Circumstance and the Action of the Noun to which it is joined by the neuter Verb, and therefore has the Property of a Participle. But if we use the same Word in a merely descriptive Sense, as, " The *writing* Master, the *trotting* Horse," it loses the Property of a Participle, and becomes a *mere Adjective*.

88. The *paſſive Participle* is, for the *moſt* Part, the *ſame* with the *preter*, or *paſt Tenſe* of the Verb; but in *both* theſe there are many *Irregularities:* the chief of which may be gathered from the following Catalogue.

| *Preſent.* | *Preter.* | *Parti.* |
|---|---|---|
| Bake | baked | baked, baken |
| Begin | began | begun |
| Bear | bore | borne |
|  | bare | born |
| Beat | beat | beaten |
| Behold | beheld | beheld |
|  |  | beholden |
| Bend | bended, bent | bent [reft |
| Bereave | bereft | bereaved, be- |
| Beſeech | beſought | beſought |
| Bid | bid | bidden |
| Bind | bound | bound |
| Bite | bit | bitten |
| Bleed | bled | bled, blooded |
| Blow | blowed | blowed |
|  | blew | blown |
| Break | broke, brake | broken |
| Breed | bred | bred |
| Bring | brought | brought |

*Preſent*

| Present. | Preter. | Parti. |
|---|---|---|
| Build | built | builded, built |
| Buy | bought | bought |
| Catch | caught | catched, catcht |
| Chide | chid, chidden | chid |
| Choose | chose | chosen |
| Cleave | clove, clave | cloven, cleft |
| Clothe | clad | clothed, clad |
| Creep | creeped, crept | creeped, crept |
| Dig | digged, dug | dug |
| Do | did | done |
| Draw | drew | drawn |
| Dream | dreamed | dreamed |
|  | dreamt | dreamt |
| Drink | drank | drunk |
| Drive | drove | driven |
| Eat | ate | eaten |
| Feed | fed | fed |
| Feel | felt | felt |
| Find | found | found |
| Fling | flung | flung |
| Forsake | forsook | forsaken |
| Freight | freighted | fraught |
| Freeze | froze | frozen |
| Get | got, gat | gotten |
| Geld | gelt | gelded |
| Gilt | gilt | gilt |
| Girt | girded, girt | girded, girt |

Give

| Present. | Preter. | Parti. |
|---|---|---|
| Give | gave | given |
| Grave | graved | graved, graven |
| Grind | ground | ground |
| Hang | hanged, hung | hanged |
| Have | had | had |
| Heave | heaved, hove | heaved, hoven |
| Help | helped | helped, holpen |
| Hew | hewed | hewn |
| Hide | hid | hidden |
| Hold | held | holden, held |
| Keep | kept | kept |
| Know | knew | known |
| Lade | laded | laden |
| Lay | laid | laid |
| Lead | led | led |
| Leap | leaped, leapt | leaped, leapt |
| Leave | left | left |
| Lend | lent | lent |
| Load | loaded | loaded, loaden |
| Lose | lost | lost |
| Make | made | made |
| Meet | met | met |
| Mow | mowed | mowed, mown |
| Rend | rent | rent |
| Ride | rid, rode | ridden |
| Ring | rang | rung |
| Rive | rived | riven |

Rot

| *Present.* | *Preter.* | *Parti.* |
|---|---|---|
| Rot | rotted | rotten |
| Run | ran | run |
| Say | said | said |
| Saw | sawed | sawn |
| See | saw | seen |
| Seek | sought | sought |
| Seeth | sod | sodden |
| Sell | sold | sold |
| Send | sent | sent |
| Shake | shook | shaken |
| Shave | shaved | shaved, shaven |
| Shear | shore | shorn |
| Shew | shewed | shewn |
| Shoe | shod | shod |
| Shoot | shot | shot |
| Shrive | shrove | shriven |
| Sing | sang | sung |
| Sink | sank | sunk |
| Sit | sate | sat, sitten |
| Slay | slew | slain |
| Sling | slung, slang | slung |
| Smite | smote | smitten |
| Sow | sowed | sown |
| Speak | spoke | spoken |
| Speed | sped | sped |
| Spell | spelt | spelt |
| Spend | spent | spent |

Spill

## GRAMMATICAL

| Present. | Preter. | Parti. |
|---|---|---|
| Spill | spilled, spilt | spilled, spilt |
| Spin | spun, span | spun |
| Spring | sprang | sprung |
| Sting | stung, stang | stung |
| Steal | stole | stolen |
| Stick | stuck | stuck |
| Stride | strode | stridden |
| Strike | struck | struck |
| String | strang | strung |
| Sweep | swept | swept |
| Swear | swore | sworn |
| Sweat | sweated | sweated |
| Swell | swelled | swoln |
| Swim | swum, swam | swum |
| Take | took | taken |
| Teach | taught | taught |
| Tear | tore | torn |
| Tell | told | told |
| Throw | threw | thrown |
| Think | thought | thought |
| Tread | trod | trodden |
| Wear | wore | worn |
| Weave | wove | woven |
| Win | won | won |
| Wind | wound | wound |
| Work | wrought | wrought |
| Wring | wrung | wrung |
| Write | wrote | written |

89. The

89. The *following* are *intransitive* Verbs, and have, properly speaking, no *passive* Participle.

| *Present.* | *Preter.* | *Parti. Form.* |
|---|---|---|
| Abide | abode | |
| Arise | arose | arisen |
| Awake | awaked, awoke | awaked |
| Cleave | cleaved, clave | cleaved |
| Cling | clang, clung | clung |
| Come | came | come |
| Creep | creeped, crept | crept |
| Crow | crew | crowed |
| Deal | dealt | dealt |
| Dare | durst | |
| Die | died | dead |
| Dwell | dwelt | dwelt |
| Fall | fell | fallen |
| Feed | fed | fed |
| Flee | fled | fled |
| Fly | flew | flown |
| Go | went | gone |
| Grow | grew | grown |
| Hang | hung | hung |
| Leap | leaped, leapt | leaped |
| Lie | lay | |
| Rise | rose | risen |
| Rot | rotted | rotten |

| Present. | Preter. | Part. Form. |
|---|---|---|
| Run | ran | run |
| Shine | shone | shined |
| Sink | sank | sunk |
| Shrink | shrank | shrunk |
| Sleep | slept | slept |
| Slide | slid | slidden |
| Slink | slank | slunk |
| Speed | sped | sped |
| Spit | spat | spitten |
| Stand | stood | stood |
| Stick | stuck | stuck |
| Stink | stank | stunk |
| Swing | swang | swung |
| Thrive | throve | thriven |
| Weep | wept | wept |

NOTE. There are a few compound irregular Verbs, such as *befal, bespeak,* &c. which as they follow the simple Form, it was not thought necessary to insert in this Catalogue.

90. There are a *few Verbs* ending in *t,* and *d*; these are the *same* in the *present, preter* Tenses, and *passive* Participle: as, burst, cast, cost, cut, hit, hurt, knit, let, put, read, rant, rid, set, shed, shred, shut, slit, split, spread, thrust.

91. Here

91. Here it may be observed, that there are *two Ways* of expressing the *perfect* and *pluperfect* Tenses in *most irregular* Verbs: as, I *have wrote*, or *have written*, &c. I *had wrote*, or *had written*, &c.

NOTE 91. In these Instances, *written*, is, I think, a real Verb, but for Distinction's Sake we call it the *participial Form;* and in all irregular Verbs it was *heretofore*, and in some of them it is *still*, the *only* Form made Use of in the *preter* Tense.

## Of an ADVERB*.

92 AN *Adverb* is a Part of Speech joined to a *Verb*, an *Adjective*, a *Participle*, and sometimes to another *Adverb*, to express the *Quality*, or *Circumstance* of it: as, He reads *well;* a *truly* good Man; he is *secretly* plotting; he writes *very correctly*.

* From *ad*, to, and *Verbum*, a Verb.

F 3     93. *Some*

93. *Some* Adverbs admit of *Comparison*: as, *often, oft'ner, oftenest; soon, sooner, soonest:* and many of them are compared by the other Adverbs, *much more, most,* &c.

NOTE. Adverbs have Relation to *Time*; as, *now, then, lat.ly,* &c.: to *Place*; as, *here, there,* &c.: to *Number;* as, *once, twice,* &c.

## Of a CONJUNCTION*.

94. A *Conjunction* is a Part of Speech that *joins* Words or Sentences, together: as, *albeit, although, altho', and, because, but, either, else, however, if, namely, neither, nor, or, though, tho' therefore, thereupon, unless, whereas, whereupon, whether, yet.*

The foregoing are *always Conjunctions:* but these six following are *sometimes Adverbs; also, as, otherwise, since, likewise, then. Except,* and *save,* are *sometimes Verbs; for,* sometimes a *Preposition;* and *that,* sometimes a *Pronoun.*

* From *con,* with, and *jungo,* to join.

*Of*

## *Of a* PREPOSITION*.

95. A *Prepofition* is a Word *fet before Nouns* or *Pronouns* to exprefs the *Relations* of Perfons, Places, or Things to each other: as, He came *to*, and ftood *before* the City.

Prepofitions ufed in this Senfe, are fuch as follow: *About, above, after, againft, among, amongft, at, before, behind, below, beneath, between, beyond, by, for, from, in, into, of, off, on, upon, over, through, to, unto, towards, under, with, within, without.*

## *Of an* INTERJECTION*.

96. AN *Interjection* is a Word that expreffes any *fudden Motion* of the Mind, *tranfported* with the Senfation of Pleafure or Pain: as, *O! Oh! Alas! Lo!*

\* From *præ*, before, and *pono*, to place.
† From *inter*, between, and *jacio*, to throw.

SYNTAX.

# SYNTAX*.

SYNTAX shews the *Agreement* and *right Disposition* of Words in a Sentence.

97. The Articles, *a*, and *an*, are used *only* before Nouns of the *singular* Number: *an*, before a Word that begins with a *Vowel*; *a*, before a Word that begins with a *Consonant:* *an*, or *a*, before a Word that begins with *h:* as, "*A* Christian, *an* Infidel, *an* "Heathen, or *a* Heathen." But if the *h* be not *sounded*, then the Article *an* is only used; as, "*An* Hour, *an* "Herb."

* From *Syntaxis*, a Joining.

# INSTITUTES. 65

98. *A* and *an* are *indefinite;* as, " *A* Man, *a* House; *i, e.* any Man, any House, without Distinction. But *the* is *definite :* as; " *The* Man, *the* House;" *i. e.* some one Man, some one House, in particular.

99. *The* is likewise used to distinguish two or more Persons or Things mentioned before; as, " *The* Men," (not the Women.) " *The* Lords," (as distinguished from the Commons.)

100. The *Verb agrees* with its *Noun*, or *Pronoun, i. e.* with its *Agent*, or *Subject,* in *Number* and *Person :* as, " The Boys *write;* I *love;* He who *reads.*

101. In the complaisant Stile, it is common to use *you,* instead of *thou* when we speak to *one* Person *only;* and

NOTE 100. This *Agent* or *Subject*, is *always* found by asking the Question *who*, or *what* on the Verb; as, *who* write? The Answer to the Question is, *Boys;* which Word is the *Agent* of the Verb *write.*

in that Case it has a *plural* Verb joined with it: as, "You *are* my Brother."

102. A Noun of *Multitude*, of the *singular* Number may have a Verb either *singular* or *plural:* as, "The People *is* mad;" or, "The People *are* mad." The latter Expression seems to be the more *elegant*.

103. When *two* or *more* Nouns, or Pronouns, are connected together in a Sentence, as *joint Agents,* or *Subjects*; they must have a *Plural* Verb, though they should be each of the *Singular* Number: as, "The Man and his Wife *are* happy; I and H *were* there; Richard and I *have been* very busy."

104. Sometimes a *Sentence*, or an *infinitive Mode*, is the *Subject* of a Verb; and then the Verb must be put in the *singular* Number and *third* Person: as, "The King and Queen appearing in public, *was* the 'cause of' my going; To see the Sun *is* pleasant."

105. When

105. When the *Agent* and *Object* of a Verb are not distinguished (as in Nouns) by *different* Cases, the *Agent* is *always* set *before*, and the *Object after* the Verb; this being the natural Order, and necessary to determine the Sense: as, " *Alexander* conquered *Darius.*" If *Darius* had been the Conqueror, it is plain that the Order of the Nouns must have been inverted.

106. The *Agent*, or *Subject*, is most commonly set *immediately before* the Verb, or the *Sign* of the Verb: as, " The *Man* lives; The *City* hath stood a thousand Years." In the *imperative* Mode, however, it is set *after* the Verb: as, " Love *thou:* Be *thou* happy." Also, when a *Question is asked,* it is set *after* the Verb, or *between* the Sign and the Verb; as, " Are *you* there? Doth the *King* live?"

107. The Pronouns, *I*, *We*, *Thou* *Ye*, *He*, *She*, *They*, and *Who*, are *always* used when they stand as the *Agent* of an *active*, or the *subject* of the *neuter* Verb: as, " *I* see; *He* loves: *We* are

are; *They* go; That is the Person *who* passed us Yesterday."

108. The *Noun* or *Pronoun*, which receives the *Force* of the *active* Verb, is most commonly set *after* the Verb, as, "I love the *Man*." But the *Relative, whom,* or *whomsoever*, is *always* set *before* the Verb: as, "The Man, *whom* I love, is absent."

109. The *accusative* Case of a Pronoun is *always* used, when it receives the *Force* or *Impression* of the *active* Verb, or *active* Participle, or comes after the *infinitive* Mode of the *neuter* Verb: as, "He calls *me*; She is beating *them;* I suppose it to be *him*."

110. When a Pronoun is set *alone* in Answer to a Question, or follows the *present* or *imperfect* Tense of the *neuter* Verb, it must be put in the *nominative* Case; as, "Who did it? *I,* i. e. *I* did it; I was *he* that said so,"

111. The *passive Participle*, and not the *past Tense,* should be *always* used when

when joined in a Sentence with the *neuter* Verb : as, " It *was written* (not it was *wrote)* in Hebrew."

112. *That* Form of the Tenses in Verbs, which is distinguished by the *active Participle,* is used with strict Propriety, when we would express the *Continuance* of an Action: as, " I *have been writing* a long Time : I *shall be writing* all the Week."

113. The *auxiliary* Signs, *do* and *did,* and their Inflections, *doth, dost,* or *does,* and *didst,* ought to be used *only* for the Sake of *Emphasis:* as, " I *do* love; He *did* go."

114. *Shall* is used in the *first* Person *barely* to express the future Action or Event; as, " I *shall* do it:" But, in he *second* and *third,* it *promises,* or comands; as, " You *shall* do it." On ? contrary, *will,* in the *second* and ·*d* Persons, *barely* expresses the fu- ·Action or Event; as, " You *will* ;" But, in the *first,* it *promises,* ·*atens ;* as; " I *will* do it."

G          115 The

115. The Terminations *eth*, *ed*, and the *participial* Form of the Verb, are used in the *grave* and *formal* Style; but *s* '*d*, and the Form of the past Tense, in the *free* and *familiar* Style: as (gravely), " He *hath loved;* The Man *hath spoken*, and still *speaketh;*" (familiarly), " He *has lov'd;* The Man *has spoke*, and still *speaks.*"

116. When *two Nouns* come together with the Preposition *of* between them, denoting *Possession*, the latter may be made the *genitive* Case, and set *before* the other: as, " The Property *of* the Men; The *Men's* Property."

117. *Pronouns* must *always agree* with the *Nouns* for which they *stand*, or to which they *refer*, in *Number*, *Person*, and *Gender*: as, " The *Sun* shines, and *his* Race is appointed to *him*; The *Moon* appears, and *she* shines with Light, but not *her* own; The *Sea* swells, *it* roars,

NOTE 115. Nouns of the *plural* Number, that end in *s*, will not very *properly* admit of the genitive Case.

and what can repel *its* Force; *This* Man, *These* Women."

118. The *neuter* Pronoun, by an Idiom peculiar to the *English* Language, is frequently joined in *explanatory* Sentences with a Noun or Pronoun of the *masculine* or *feminine* Gender: as, "*It* is *I*; *It* was the *Man*, or *Woman* that did it."

119. When *two* or *more* Nouns or Pronouns, of *different Persons*, are joined in a Sentence, the Pronoun, which refers to them, must agree with the *first* Person in Preference to the *second*, and with the *second* in Preference to the *third*: as, ' *Thou* and thy *Father* are both in the same Fault, and *ye* ought to confess it; The *Captain* and *I* fought on the same Ground, and after-

NOTE 118. Though this seems to be an *indefinitive* Use of the *neuter* Pronoun, as expressive of some Cause or Subject of Inquiry, without any Respect to *Person* or *Gender*; yet, in strict Propriety, it cannot be so used with a Noun of the Plural Number: thus, " *It* was *they* that did it," is an Impropriety.

wards *we* divided the Spoil, and shared it between *us*."

120. When *two* or *more* Nouns or Pronouns of the *singular* Number are joined together in a Sentence, the Pronoun which refers to them, must be of the *plural* Number: as, "The *King* and the *Queen* had put on *their* Robes."

121. The *genitive* Case of a Pronoun is *always* used, when joined to a Noun, to denote *Property* or *Possession:* as, "*My* Head and *thy* Hand." The Head of *me* and the Hand of *thee* are inelegant Expressions.

122. The *genitive* Cases of the Pronouns, viz. *my*, *thy*, &c. are used when joined with Nouns; but *mine*, *thine*, &c. when put *absolutely*, or *without* their Nouns: as, "It is *my* Book;" or, omitting the Noun, "It is *mine*."

The same Thing may be observed of *other* and *others*, in the *plural* Number: as, "The Property of *other* Men;" or, without

without the Noun, "the Property of *others*."

123. *Mine* and *thine* are frequently put for *my* and *thy*, before a Word that begins with a *Vowel*: as, "*Mine* Eye" for "*My* Eye."

124. *Pronominal Adjectives* are only used in the *genitive* Case, when put *absolutely*: as, "I will not do it for *ten's* Sake."

125. The *Adjective* is usually set *before* its *Substantive*: as, "The *second* Year; A *good* Man." Sometimes, however, for better Sound's Sake, especially in Poetry, the Adjective comes *after* its Substantive: as,

"The genuine Cause of every Deed divine."

NOTE 123. *Thou* is used to denote the *greatest Respect*: as, "O *Thou* most high!" And likewise to denote the *greatest Contempt*: as, "*Thou* worthless Fellow!"

126. When *Thing* or *Things* is Substantive to an Adjective, the Word *Thing* or *Things* is elegantly omitted, and the Adjective is put *absolutely*, or *without* its *Substantive:* as, "Who will shew us any *Good?*" for, "Who will shew us any *good Thing?*"

In many *other* Cases the Adjective is put *absolutely*, especially when the Noun has been mentioned before, and is easily understood, though not expressed.

127. In forming the *Degrees of Comparison*, the Adverbs, *more, most, less, least,* &c. are *only* used before Adjectives when the Terminations, *er* and *est*, are omitted: as, "More full, *less* beautiful."

128. For better Sound's Sake, most Adjectives ending in *ive, al, ful, ble, ant, some, ing, ish, ous,* and some others, must be compared by the Adverbs *more, most, less, least,* &c. as, "Pensive, *more* pensive; substantial, *more* substantial."

NOTE 128. Adjectives of more than one syllable generally come under this Rule.

129. When two *Persons*, or *Things*, are spoken of in a Sentence, and there is Occasion to mention them over again, for the Sake of Distinction, *that* is used in Reference to the *former*, and *this* in Reference to the *latter*: as,

"*Self love*, the Spring of Motion, acts the Soul;
"*Reason's comparing Balance* rules the whole:
"Man but for *that* no Action could attend,
"And but for *this* were active to no End."

130. That refers both to *Persons* and *Things*: as, "The Man *that* I respect; The Thing *that* I want, is not here."

131. The relative Pronoun, *who*, *whose*, or *whom*, is used, when we speak of Persons *only*; *which*, when we speak of Things, or want to distinguish one of two or more Persons or Things: as, "I am bound to respect a *Man*, *who* has done me a Favor; though he be chargeable

able with *Vices, which* I hate. *Which* of the Men? *Which* of the Roads will you choose?"

132. *Who* and *what* also are used in asking Questions: *who*, when we inquire for a Man's Name; as, "*Who* is that Man?" *What*, when we would know his Occupation, &c. as, "*What* is that Man?"

133. The *Adverb* is *always* placed *immediately before* the Adjective, but *most commonly after* the Verb: as, "A *very* pious Man prays *frequently.*"

134. The *Comparative* Adverbs *than* and *as*, with the Conjunctions *and, nor, or*, connect like Cases: as, "She loves him better *than me; John* is as tall *as I; He and I* went together; Neither *he nor she* came; Bring it to *me or her.*"

135. The *Conjunctions, if, though except*, &c. implying a *manifest Doubt* or *Uncertainty*, require the *subjunctive* Form of Verbs: as, "Though he *slay* me,

me, yet will I trust in him; I will not let thee go, except thou *bless* me; Kiss the Son, lest he *be* angry; If he but *speak* the Word: See thou *do* it not."

136. *Prepositions always* govern the *accusative* Case of a Pronoun *immediately after* them; as, "To *me*, for *them*," &c.

137. After Verbs of *shewing, giving,* &c. the Preposition, *to*, is *elegantly omitted* before the Pronoun, which notwithstanding, *must* be in the *Accusative:* as "I gave him the Book," for "I gave *to* him the Book."

138. The Preposition, *to*, is *always* used *before* Nouns of *Place,* after Verbs and Participles of *Motion:* as, "I went *to* London; I am going *to* Town," &c. But the Preposition *at*, is *always* used when it *follows* the *neuter* Verb in the

NOTE 135. This Form seems to be *elliptical,* and may be thus resolved: " Though he *should* slay me: Lest he *should* be angry: See thou *must* do it not," &c.

same

same Case: as, "I have been *at London*; I am *at* the Place appointed." We likewise say, "He touch'd, arriv'd, lives, &c. *at* any Place."

139. The Preposition *in*. is set before *Countries, Cities*. and *large* Towns, especially if they are in the *same* Nation: as, "He lives *in London, in France*, &c." *At* is set before *Villages*, *single* Houses, and *Cities* that are in *distant* Countries: as, "He lives *at Hackney*, &c."

140. The *Interjections, O. Oh,* and *Ah,* require the *accusative* Case of a Pronoun in the *first* Person: as, "O *me*, Oh *me*, Ah *me*:" But the *nominative* in the *second*: as, "O *thou*, O *ye*."

No *exact* Rules can be given for the placing of *all* Words in a Sentence: The *easy Flow* and the *Perspicuity* of the Expression are the *two Things*, which ought to be *chiefly* regarded.

## APPENDIX.

# APPENDIX.

The DECLENSION of IRREGULAR AND DEFECTIVE VERBS.

## TO WRITE.

*Present.*    *Preter.*    *Part.*
WRITE    Wrote    Written.

### INDICATIVE MODE.

*Imperfect Tense.*

Sing. I wrote or did write, thou wrotest or didst write, he wrote or did write. Plu. We wrote or did write, ye wrote or did write, they wrote or did write.

*Perfect*

*Perfect Tense.*

*Sing.* I have wrote or have written, thou hast wrote or hast written, he hath or has wrote, or hath or has written. *Plu.* We have wrote or have written, ye have wrote or have written, they have wrote or have written.

*Pluperfect Tense.*

*Sing.* I had wrote or had written, thou hadst wrote or hadst written, he had wrote or had written. *Plu.* We had wrote or had written, ye had wrote or had written, they had wrote or had written.

INFINITIVE MODE.

*Perfect Tense.*

To have wrote or to have written.

POTENTIAL MODE.

*Perfect and pluperfect Tenses.*

*Sing.* I might have wrote or written, thou mightest have wrote or written, he,

he might have wrote or written. *Plu.*
We might have wrote or written, ye might have wrote or written, they might have wrote or written.

The other Modes and Tenses follow the regular Form.

## TO SEE.

*Present.*       *Preter.*       *Parti.*
See              Saw             Seen.

### INDICATIVE MODE.

*Imperfect Tense.*
*Sing.* I saw or did see, thou sawest or didst see, he saw or did see. *Plu.* We saw or did see, ye saw or did see, they saw or did see.

*Perfect Tense.*
*Sing.* I have seen, thou hast seen, hath or has seen. *Plu.* We have seen, ye have seen, they have seen.

H                POTEN-

## POTENTIAL MODE.

*Perfect and p'uperfect Tenses.*

*Sing.* I might have seen, thou mightest have seen, he might have seen. *Plu.* We might have seen, ye might have seen, they might have seen.

## INFINITIVE MODE.

*Perfect Tense.*

To have seen.

This is one of those Verbs in which the perfect Tenses must be expressed by the *participial* Form: And which, I think, is always the Case when that Form consists but of one Syllable.

## TO GO.

| *Pres.* | *Preter.* | *Parti. Form.* |
|---------|-----------|----------------|
| Go      | Went,     | Gone.          |

## INDICATIVE MODE.

### *Imperfect Tense.*

*Sing.* I went or did go, thou wentest or didst go, he went or did go. *Plu.* We went or did go, ye went or did go, they went or did go.

### *Perfect Tense.*

*Sing.* I have gone, thou hast gone, he hath or has gone. *Plu.* We have gone, ye have gone, they have gone.

### *Pluperfect Tense.*

*Sing.* I had gone, thou hadst gone, he had gone. *Plu.* We had gone, ye had gone, they had gone.

## POTENTIAL MODE.

### *Perfect Tense.*

*Sing.* I might have gone, thou mightest have gone, he might have gone. *Plu.* We might have gone, ye might have gone, they might have gone.

## INFINITIVE MODE.

### *Perfect Tense.*

To have gone.

The *participial Form* of this Verb is often joined to the Neuter Verb, when it refers to the mere Circumstance or Event of Going: as, "He *is just gone:* He has *been gone* some time." The same Thing may be observed of the Verb, *to come.*

## TO SHINE.

| *Present.* | *Preter.* | *Parti. Form* |
|---|---|---|
| Shine | Shone | Shined. |

## INDICATIVE MODE.

### *Imperfect Tense.*

*Sing.* I shone or did shine, thou didst shine, he shone or did shine. *Plu.* We shone or did shine, ye shone or did shine, they shone or did shine.

*Perfect*

*Perfect Tense.*

*Sing.* I have shone or have shined, thou hast shone or hast shined, he hath shone or hath or has shined. *Plu.* We have shone or have shined, ye have shone or have shined, they have shone or have shined.

*Pluperfect Tense.*

*Sing.* I had shone or had shined, thou hadst shone or hadst shined, he had shone or had shined. *Plu.* We had shone or had shined, ye had shone or had shined, they had shone or had shined.

POTENTIAL MODE.

*Perfect Tense.*

*Sing.* I might have shone or shined, thou mightest have shone or shined, he might have shone or shined. *Plu.* We might have shined, &c.

INFINITIVE MODE.

*Perfect Tense.*

To have shone or to have shined.

Though

Though this Verb has, properly speaking, no *paffive* Participle, yet it has a *participial* Form as above, which is used in the perfect Tenses, and in this it agrees with other Verbs of the same Class.

## TO LET.

(Signifying to permit or suffer.)

*Present.*        *Preter.*
Let             Let.

### INDICATIVE MODE.

*Present Tense.*

*Sing.* I let, thou lettest, he letteth or lets. *Plu.* We let, ye let, they let.

*Imperfect Tense.*

*Sing.* I did let, thou didst let, he did let. *Plu.* We did let, ye did let, they did let.

*Perfect Tense.*

*Sing.* I have let, thou hast let, he hath or has let. *Plu.* We have let, ye have let, they have let.

*Plu.*

# APPENDIX.

*Pluperfect Tense.*

*Sing.* I had let, thou hadst let, he had let. *Plu.* We had let, ye had let, they had let.

*Future Tense.*

*Sing.* I will let, thou wilt let, he will let. *Plu.* We will let, ye will let, they will let.

## IMPERATIVE MODE.

*Sing.* Let, or do thou let. *Plu.* Let, or do ye let.

## POTENTIAL MODE.

*Present and future Tenses.*

*Sing.* I may let, thou mayest let, he may let. *Plu.* We may let, ye may let, they may let.

*Perfect Tense.*

*Sing.* I might have let, thou mightest have let, he might have let. *Plu.* We might

might have let, ye might have let, they might have let.

## INFINITIVE MODE.

*Pref.* To let.  *Pret.* To have let.
*Fut.* About to let.

This shews that *Let* is not a Sign of the imperative Mode, but a real Verb, occasionally used in all Modes and Tenses, joined to some other Verb in the infinitive Mode, either expressed or understood: as, " You will *let* me do it, I might have *let* him go."

*Let*, signifying *to let down*, &c. may have a *passive* Participle: as, " I was *let, down* in a Basket."

## TO DARE.

(Signifying to venture.)

| *Present.* | *Preter.* |
|---|---|
| Dare | Durst |

INDI-

# APPENDIX. 89

## Indicative Mode.

*Present Tense.*
*Sing.* I dare, thou dareſt, he dareth or dares. *Plu.* We dare, ye dare, they dare.

*Imperfect Tenſe.*
*Sing.* I durſt, thou durſt, he durſt. *Plu.* We durſt, ye durſt, they durſt or did dare.

*Perfect and pluperfect Tenſes.*
*Sing.* I durſt have, thou durſt have, he durſt have. *Plu.* We durſt have, ye durſt have, they durſt have.

*Future Tenſe.*
*Sing.* I will dare, thou wilt dare, he will dare. *Plu.* We will dare, ye will dare, they will dare.

*Imperatively.*
Dare do it.

*Interrogatively.*
Dare you do it?

The Verb *Ought* is only used in the Indicative.

*Present and future Tenses.*

*Sing.* I ought, thou oughtest, he ought. *Plu.* We ought, ye ought, they ought.

*Preter Tense.*

*Sing.* I ought to have, thou oughtest to have, he ought to have. *Plu.* We ought to have, ye ought to have, they ought to have.

These two last defective Verbs are used only as above, and always joined to another Verb expressed or understood in the infinitive Mode; as, " I *durst* have done it. I *dare* say. Some would even *dare* to die. I *ought* to love you. I *ought* to have gone thither."

DARE (to provoke) is regular.

WOT (to know) and QUOTH (to say) are very defective.

Ind-

# APPENDIX.  91

### Indicative Mode.

*Present Tense.*

I wot            He wotteth
They wot         Wot ye?

*Preter Tense.*

I wist           He wist
They wist        Wist ye

Quoth I          Quoth he.

These two last Verbs are seldom used by late Writers.

## An Easy

### Praxis on Gen. xlv. 1, &c.

### Verse 1.

| | |
|---|---|
| THEN | an Adverb |
| Joseph | a Substantive |
| could | a Sign of the Potential Mode |
| not | an Adverb |
| refrain | a Verb |
| himself | a Pronouon |
| before | a Preposition |
| all | an Adjective |
| them | a Pronoun |
| that | a Pronoun |
| stood | a Verb |
| by | a Preposition |
| him | a Pronoun |
| and | a Conjunction |
| he | a Pronoun |
| cried | a Verb |
| cause | a Verb |

every

| | |
|---|---|
| every | an Adjective |
| man | a Substantive |
| to | a Sign of the Infinitive Mode |
| go | a Verb |
| out | an Adverb |
| from | a Preposition |
| me | a Pronoun |
| and | a Conjunction |
| there | an Adverb |
| stood | a Verb |
| no | an Adjective |
| man | a Substantive |
| with | a Preposition |
| him | a Pronoun |
| while | an Adverb |
| Joseph | a Substantive |
| made | a Verb |
| himself | a Pronoun |
| known | a Participle |
| unto | a Preposition |
| his | a Pronoun |
| brethren | a Substantive |

Verse 2.

| | |
|---|---|
| And | a Conjunction |
| he | a Pronoun |
| wept | |

| | |
|---|---|
| wept | a Verb |
| aloud | an Adverb |
| and | a Conjunction |
| the | an Article |
| Egyptians | a Substantive |
| and | a Conjunction |
| the | an Article |
| house | a Substantive |
| of | a Preposition |
| Pharaoh | a Substantive |
| heard | a Verb |

### Verse 3.

| | |
|---|---|
| And | a Conjunction |
| Joseph | a Substantive |
| said | a Verb |
| unto | a Preposition |
| his | a Pronoun |
| brethren | a Substantive |
| I | a Pronoun |
| am | a Verb |
| Joseph | a Substantive |
| doth | a Sign of the present Tense |
| my | a Pronoun |
| father | a Substantive |
| yet | an Adverb |
| | live |

# APPENDIX.

| | |
|---|---|
| live | a Verb |
| and | a Conjunction |
| his | a Pronoun |
| brethren | a Substantive |
| could | a Sign of the Potential Mode |
| not | an Adverb |
| answer | a Verb |
| him | a Pronoun |
| for | a Conjunction |
| they | a Pronoun |
| were | a Verb |
| troubled | a Participle |
| at | a Preposition |
| his | a Pronoun |
| presence | a Substantive |

### Verse 4.

| | |
|---|---|
| And | a Conjunction |
| Joseph | a Substantive |
| said | a Verb |
| unto | a Preposition |
| his | a Pronoun |
| brethren | a Substantive |
| come | a Verb |
| near | an Adverb |
| to | a Preposition |
| me | a Pronoun |

I              a Pronoun
pray           a Verb
you            a Pronoun
and            a Conjunction
they           a Pronoun
came           a Verb
near           an Adverb
and            a Conjunction
he             a Pronoun
said           a Verb
I              a Pronoun
am             a Verb
Joseph         a Substantive
your           a Pronoun
brother        a Substantive
whom           a Pronoun
ye             a Pronoun
fold           a Verb
into           a Prepofition
Egypt          a Substantive

        Verfe 5.
Now            an Adverb
therefore      an Adverb
be             a Verb
not            an Adverb
grieved        a Participle

# APPENDIX.

| | |
|---|---|
| nor | a Conjunction |
| angry | an Adjective |
| with | a Preposition |
| yourselves | a Pronoun |
| that | a Conjunction |
| ye | a Pronoun |
| sold | a Verb |
| me | a Pronoun |
| hither | an Adverb |
| for | a Conjunction |
| God | a Substantive |
| did | a Sign of the Imperfect Tense |
| send | a Verb |
| me | a Pronoun |
| before | a Preposition |
| you | a Pronoun |
| to | a Sign of the Infinitive Mode |
| preserve | a Verb |
| life | a Substantive |

### Verse 6.

| | |
|---|---|
| For | a Conjunction |
| these | a Pronoun |
| two | an Adjective |
| years | |

| | |
|---|---|
| years | a Substantive |
| hath | a Sign of the perfect Tense |
| the | an Article |
| famine | a Substantive |
| been | a Verb |
| in | a Preposition |
| the | an Article |
| 'and | a Substantive |
| and | a Conjunction |
| yet | an Adverb |
| there | an Adverb |
| are | a Verb |
| five | an Adjective |
| years | a Substantive |
| in | a Preposition |
| the | an Article |
| which | a Pronoun |
| there | an Adverb |
| shall | a Sign of the future Tense |
| neither | a Conjunction |
| be | a Verb |
| earing | a Substantive |
| nor | a Conjunction |
| harvest | a Substantive. |

# APPLICATION

OF THE

Grammatical Inſtitutes.

For the Uſe of thoſe who may want the Aſſiſtance of a Maſter.

---

Part of DAVID's Speech to GOLIATH the Philiſtine.

—Thou comeſt—

THOU, *a Pronoun* 23; *ſing. Number*, 4; *nom. Caſe*, 24; *the Agent of the Verb*, 107; *the ſecond Perſon*, 55. Comeſt, *a Verb*, 29; *irregular*, 89; *indicative Mode*, 33; *preſent Tenſe*, 38; *ſing. Number and ſecond Perſon*, 55; *agreeing with its Agent,*
Thou

—to me with a Sword, and with a Spear, and with a Shield: But I come to thee—

Thou, 100. To, *a Preposition*, 95. Me, *a Pronoun*, 23; *accusative Case,* 24; *following a Preposition*, 136. With *a Preposition*, 95. A. *an Article,* 2; *set before a Noun of the singular Number, and a Word beginning with a Consonant,* 97. Sword, *a Noun, or Substantive,* 3. And, *a Conjunction,* 94. Spear, and Shield, *Nouns, signifying Things,* 3. But, *a Conjunction,* 94. I, *a Pronoun,* 23; *sing. Number,* 4; *the nominative Case,* 24; *the Agent of the Verb,* 107; *the first Peson,* 54. Come, *a Verb,* 29; *irregular,* 89; *indicative Mode,* 33; *present Tense,* 38; *first Person sing. Number.* 53; *agreeing with its Agent,* I, 100. Thee, *a Pronoun,* 23; *sing. Number,* 4; *accusative Case,* 24; *following*

NOTE. *The same Word occurring a second or third Time, &c. is but once explained, except it has a different Construction.*

*a Pre-*

—in the Name of the Lord of Hosts, the God of the Armies of Israel, whom thou hast defied. This Day will the Lord deliver—

*a* Preposition, 136. In *a* Preposition, 95. The *an* Article. 2. Name, *a Noun,* 3. Of, *a Preposition,* 95. Lord, *a Noun, referring to a Person,* 3. Hosts, *a Noun,* 3; *plural Number,* 4; *so made by adding* s *to the Singular,* 5. God, *a Noun, referring to a Person,* 3. Armies, *a Noun,* 3; *plural Number,* 4; *so made by changing* y *into* ies, 7. Whom, *a Pronoun,* 23; *referring to a Person,* 131; *accusative Case,* 25; *receiving the Force of the Verb,* Defied, 109. Hast an *Auxiliary Sign, denoting the perfect Tense,* 50. Defied, *a Verb,* 29; *indicative Mode,* 33; *perfect Tense,* 40; *formed by adding* d *to the first Person, singular,* 44; *second Person singular Number,* 55; *agreeing with its* Agent, Thou, 100. This, *a Pronoun,* 23. Day, *a Noun,* 3. Will, *a Sign of the future Tense,* 52. Deliver, *a Verb,* 29; *indicative Mode,* 33; *future Tense,* 42; *singular Number*

—thee into my Hand, and I will take thy Head from thee.

*ber*, *and third Person*, 56; *agreeing with its Agent*, Lord, 100. Thee, *a Pronoun*, 23; *accusative Case*, 24; *receiving the Force of the active Verb*, Deliver, 109. Into *a Proposition* 95. My, *a Pronoun*, 23; *singular Number*, 4; *genitive Case*, 24; *denoting Possession*, 121. Hand, *a Noun signifying a Thing*, 3. Take, *a Verb*, 29; *irregular*, 88; *indicative Mode*, 33; *future Tense*, 42; *first Person singular*, 54; *agreeing with its Agent*, I, 100. Thy, *a Pronoun*, 23; *genitive Case*, 24; *denoting Possession*, 121; *singular Number*, 4; *joined with a Noun*, 122. Head, *a Noun*, 3. From *a Preposition*, 95. Thee, *a Pronoun*, 23; *accusative Case*, 24; *following a Preposition*, 136.

The Conclusion of PRIAM's Speech to ACHILLES, when he begged the Body of his Son HECTOR.

Think of thy Father, and this Face
    behold:
See him in me, as—

Think, *a Verb*, 29; *irregular*, 88; *imperative Mode*, 34; *singular Number and second Person*, 55; *agreeing with its Agent*, Achilles, *understood* 100. Of, *a Preposition*, 95. Thy, *a Pronoun*, 23, *as before*. Father, *a Noun*, 3. And, *a Conjunction*, 94. This, *a Pronoun*, 23. Face, *a Noun* 3. Behold *a Verb*, 29; *irregular*, 88; *same Mode*, &c. *with* Think. See, *a Verb irregular, same as* Behold. Him, *a Pronoun*, 23; *accusative Case*, 24; *receiving the Force of the Verb*, See, 109. In, *a Preposition*, 95; Me, *a Pronoun*, 23; *accusative Case*, 24; *coming after a Preposition*, 136. As,
*an*

———————helpless and as old!
Tho' not so wretched: There he yields
    to me,
The first of Men in sovereign Misery,
Thus forc'd to kneel,—

*an Adverb* 92. Wretched, *an Adjective, signifying the Quality of a Person,* 18. There, *an Adverb* 92. He, *a Pronoun,* 23; *singular Number,* 4; *nominative Case,* 24; *the Agent of a Verb,* 108. Yields, *a Verb* 29; *indicative Mode,* 33; *present Tense,* 38; *third Person singular, formed by adding s to the first Person singular,* 53; *agreeing with its Agent,* He, 100. To, *a Preposition,* 95. Me, *a Pronoun,* 23; *accusative Case,* 24; *following a Preposition,* 136. The, *an Article,* 2. First, *an Adjective,* 18. Of, *a Preposition,* 95. Men, *a Noun,* 3; *plural Number* 4; *formed by changing the Vowel,* 8. Sovereign, *an Adjective,* 18; *one that must be compared by the Adverbs,* 128. Misery, *a Noun,* 3. Thus, *an Adverb,* 92. Forced, *a passive Participle from the Verb,* Force, *by adding* d, 87. To, *a Sign of the infinitive Mode,* 46. Kneel, *a Verb,* 29; *infinitive*

—Thus groveling to embrace
The Scourge and Ruin of my Realm
  and Race,
Suppliant my Children's Murderer to
  implore,
And kiſs thoſe Hands yet reeking—


*tive Mode,* 36. Groveling, *an active Particle formed from the Verb,* grovel, *by adding* ing, 87. Embrace, *a Verb,* 29; *infinitive Mode,* 36. Scourge, Ruin, *Nouns,* 3. My, *Pronoun,* 23; *genitive Caſe denoting Poſſeſſion,* 121; *joined to a Noun,* 122. Realm, Race, *Nouns,* 3. Suppliant, *Adjective,* 18; *one that muſt be compared by the Adverbs,* 128. Children's, *Noun,* 3; *genitive Caſe,* 116; *formed by adding s to the nominative* 17. Murderer, *Noun.* 3. Implore, *Verb,* 29: *infinitive Mode,* 36; Kiſs, *Verb,* 29; *infinitive Mode,* 36; *following the Sign,* To, *underſtood.* Thoſe, *Pronoun,* 23; *plural Number,* 26. Hands, *Noun, plural Number,* 3. Yet, *Adverb,* 92. Reeking, *active Participle formed by adding* ing, *to the Verb*

—With their Gore.

*Pope's Homer.*

Verb, 87. With, *Preposition*, 95. Their *Pronoun*, 23; *Genitive Case*, 24; referring to a Noun of the plural Number, 117; joined with a Noun, 122. Gore, a Noun signifying a Thing, 3.

*Part*

# APPENDIX. 107

*Part of* Adam's *Speech to* Eve.

Sole Partner and sole Part of all these Joys!
Dearer thyself than all! needs must the Power
That made—

Sole, *Adjective*, 18; *set before its Noun;* 125. Partner, *Noun*, 3. And, *Conjunction*, 94. Part, *Noun*, 3. Of, *Preposition*, 95. All, *Adjective*, 18. These, *Pronoun*, 23; *plural Number,* 26. Joys, *Noun*, 3; *plural,* 4; *by adding* s, 5. Dearer, *Adjective*, 18; *comparative Degree,* 19; *formed by adding* er, *to the positive,* 20. Thyself, *Pronoun,* 26. Than, *Adverb,* 92; *used in Comparison,* 134. Needs, *Adverb,* 92. Must, *Sign of the potential Mode,* 47. The, *Article,* 2. Power, *Noun,* 3. That, *Pronoun,* 23. Made, *Verb,* 29; *irregular,* 84; *indicative Mode,* 33; *perfect Tense,* 40; *singular*

—us, and for us this ample World,
Be infinitely Good ——.

MILTON.

*singular Number and third Person*, 53 *agreeing with its Agent*, That, 100. Us, a *Pronoun*, 23, *plural Number* 4; *accusative Case*, 24; *receiving the Force of the Verb*, Made, 109. For, *Preposition*, 95. Us, *Pronoun*, 23; *accusative Case* 24; *following a Preposition*, 136. This, *Pronoun*, 23; *singular Number*, 26. Ample, *Adjective*, 18; *set before its Noun*, 125. World, *Noun*, 3. Be, *Verb neuter*, 30; *potential Mode, following the Sign of that Mode*. Must, 35; *singular Number and third Person*, 53; *agreeing with its Agent*, Power, 100. Infinitely, *Adverb*, 92; *set before its Adjective*, 133. Good, *Adjective*, 18; *peculiar in its Comparison*, 22.

# APPENDIX.

*Part of* Adam *and* Eve's *Morning Hymn.*

These are thy glorious Works, Parent
   of Good!
Almighty! Thine———

These, *Pronoun, plural Number,* 26. Are, *a Verb neuter,* 30; *indicative Mode,* 33; *present Tense,* 38; *plural Number, and third Person,* 53; *agreeing with its Subject,* Works, 100. Thy, *Pronoun,* 23; *genitive Case,* 24; *referring to a Noun of the singular Number,* 117; *joined with a Noun,* 122. Works, *a Noun,* 3; *plural Number,* 4; *so made by adding* s, *to the singular,* 5. Glorious, *Ajective,* 18; *one that must be compared by the Adverbs,* 128; *set before its Noun,* 125. Parent, *Noun,* 3. Of, *Preposition,* 95. Good, *Adjective,* 18; *put absolutely, the Word,* Things, *being understood,* 126. Almighty, *Adjective,* 18. Thine, *Pronoun,* 23; *genitive Case, denoting Possession,* 121; *put without the Noun immediately following,* 122.

———this univerſal Frame.
—Thyſelf—
To us inviſible or dimly ſeen
In theſe thy loweſt Works.
Speak ye who—

122. This, *Pronoun*, 23. Univerſal, *Adjective*, 18; *one that muſt be compared by the Adverbs*, 128. Frame, *Noun*, 3. Thyſelf, *Pronoun*, 23. To, *Prepoſition*, 95. Us, *Pronoun*, 23; *plural Number*, 4; *accuſative Caſe*, 24; *following a Prepoſition*, 136. Inviſible, *Adjective*, 18; *one that muſt be compared by the Adverbs*, 128. Or, *Conjunction*, 94. Dimly *Adverb*, 92. Seen, *paſſive Participle*, 87, *from the irregular Verb*, See, 88. In, *Prepoſition*, 95. Theſe, *Pronoun*, *plural Number*, 26. Loweſt, *Adjective*, 18; *ſuperlative Degree, formed by adding* elt, *to the poſitive State*, 20. Speak, *Verb*, 29; *irregular*, 84; *imperative Mode*, 34; *plural Number and ſecond Perſon*, 53; *agreeing with its Agent*, Ye, 100. Ye, *Pronoun*. 23; *plural Nnmber*, 4; *nominative Caſe*, 24; *the Agent of a Verb*, 107. Who, *Pronoun*, 23; *referring to a Perſon*, 131; *nominative Caſe*, 25;

*the*

# APPENDIX.

―best can tell, ye Sons of Light.
Angels! for ye behold him―
Thou Sun!
Acknowledge him thy greater!

*the Agent of a Verb*, 107. Best, *Adverb,* 92; *peculiar in its Comparison, and superlative Degree,* 93. Can, *Sign of the potential Mode,* 47. Tell, *Verb,* 29; *irregular,* 84; *potential Mode,* 35; *present Tense,* 38; *Plural Number, second Person,* 53; *agreeing with its Agent,* Ye, 100. Sons, Light, Angels, *Nouns,* 3. For, *Conjunction,* 94. Behold, *Verb,* 29; *irregular,* 84; *indicative Mode,* 33; *present Tense,* 38; *plural Number, second Person,* 53; *agreeing with its Agent,* Ye, 100. Him, *Pronoun,* 23; *singular Number,* 4; *accusative Case,* 24; *receiving the Force of the active Verb,* Behold, 109. Thou, *Pronoun,* 23; *singular Number,* 4: *nominative Case,* 24; *the Agent to a Verb,* 107. Sun, *Noun,* 3; *masculine Gender,* 15. Acknowledge, *Verb,* 29; *imperative Mode,* 34; *singular Number, second Person,* 53; *agreeing with its Agent.* Sun, 100. Greater, *Adjective,* 18; *comparative Degree* 19; *formed by adding* er, *to the positive State,* 20.

Air, and ye Elements! the eldest Birth
Of Nature's Womb—
———Ye Birds,———
Bear on your Wings, and in your Notes
his Praise.
Hail universal Lord! be—

20. Air, Elements, *Nouns,* 3. The, *Article,* 2. Eldest, *Adjective,* 18; *Superlative Degree,* 19; *peculiar in its Comparison,* 22; *set before its Noun,* 125. Birds, *Noun,* 3; *plural Number,* 4; *formed by adding* s *to the singular* 5; *second Person,* 53. Bear, *Verb,* 29; *irregular,* 84; *imperative Mode,* 35; *plural Number and second Person,* 53; *agreeing with its Agent,* Birds, 100. On, *Preposition,* 95. Your, *Pronoun,* 23; *genitive Case, denoting Possession,* 121; *referring to a Noun of the plural Number,* 117. Wings, *Noun,* 3; *plural Number,* 4; *so made by adding* s *to the singular,* 5. And, *Conjunction,* 94. In, *Preposition,* 95. Notes, *Noun,* 3. His, *Pronoun,* 23; *referring to a Noun of the masculine Gender,* 117. Hail, *a Verb used only in Salutation,* 29. Lord, *Noun,* 3. Be, *Verb neuter,* 30; *imperative Mode*
34;

———bounteous ftill
To give us only Good;— [*Milton.*]

34; *fingular Number, fecond Perfon*, 53; *agreeing with its Subject*, Lord, 100. Bounteous, *an Adjective*, 18: *one that muft be compared by the Adverbs*, 128. Still, *an Adverb*, 92. To, *Sign of the infinitive Mode*, 46. Give, *Verb*, 29; *irregular*, 84; *infinitive Mode*, 36. Us, *Pronoun*, 23; *plural Number*, 4; *accufative Cafe*, 24; *governed of the Prepofition*, to, *fuppreffed after a Verb of Giving*, &c. 137. Only, *Adverb*, 92. Good, *Adjective*, 18: *peculiar in its Comparifon*, 22; *fet abfolutely, the Word*, Things, *being underflood*, 126.

NOTE, Though the *proper Ufe* of a *Conjunction* is to *connect* the Parts of a Difcourfe *together*, and of an *Adverb to exprefs fome Circumftances* of an *Action*, &c. yet in *fome* Inftances, the *fame Word* may feem to anfwer *both thefe Purpofes;* in which Cafe it is not very material, whether we call it an *Adverb*, or a *Conjunction*.

OF

## OF THE ELLIPSIS.

ELLIPSIS, as applied to Grammar, is the Omission of some Word or Words which must be supplied, either to complete the Sense, or to make out the grammatical Construction of the Sentence.

The principal Design of Ellipsis is to avoid disagreeable Repititions, as well as to express our Ideas in as few Words, and as pleasing a Manner as possible.

In the application of this Figure, great Care should be taken to avoid Ambiguity; for whenever it obscures the Sense, it ought by no Means to be admitted.

Almost all compound Sentences are more or less elliptical.

# APPENDIX.

*The* ELLIPSES *of the* ARTICLE.

"*A* Man, Woman, and Child, i. e.
"*A* Man, *a* Woman, and *a* Child."

"*A* Father and Son. *The* Sun and
"Moon. *The* Day and Hour."

In all which Inſtances the Article being once mentioned, the Repitition of it, unleſs ſome peculiar Emphaſis requires it, would be unneceſſary.

"Not only the Year, but *the* Day,
and *the* Hour."

In this Caſe the Ellipſis of the laſt Article would be rather improper.

*The* ELLIPSES *of the* NOUN.

"A learned, wiſe, and good *Man*:
"i. e. A learned *Man*, and a wiſe *Man*,
"and a good *Man*."

"A prudent and faithful *Wife*. The
"*Laws* of God and Man. The Safety
"and Happineſs of the *State*."

In

In some very emphatical Expressions the Ellipsis should not be admitted; as, "Christ the Power of God, and the "Wisdom of God."

" At Saint *James*'s.
" By Saint *Paul*'s."

Here we have a Noun in the genitive Case, and no Word in the Sentence to govern it; the Ellipsis must therefore be supplied to make out the Construction: And yet, in common Conversation at least, it is much better to say, " I went by Saint *Paul*'s." than " I went by Saint *Paul*'s *Church*."

*The* ELLIPSIS *of the* ADJECTIVE.

" A *delightful* Orchard and Garden, " i. e. A *delightful* Orchard and a *delightful* Garden."

" A *little* Man and Woman, *Great* " Wealth and Power."

In such elliptical Expressions, the Adjective ought to have exactly the same
Signifi-

Signification, and to be quite as proper, when joined to the latter as to the former Subſtantives; otherwiſe the Ellipſis ſhould not be admitted.

Nor ſhould we, I think, apply this Ellipſis of the Adjective to Nouns of *different* Numbers.

"A *magnificent* Houſe and Gardens." Better uſe another Word." A *magnifi-* " *cent* Houſe and *fine* Gardens."

" A tall Man and a Woman."

In this Sentence there is no Ellipſis; the Adjective or Quality reſpects only the Man.

*The* ELLIPSIS *of the* PRONOUN.

" *I* love and fear *Him*, i. e. *I* love " *Him*, and *I* fear *Him*."

" *My* Houſe and Lands. *Thy* Learn " ing and Wiſdom. *His* Wife an - " Daughter. *Her* Lord and Maſter,"d

L  In

# APPENDIX.

In all thefe Inftances the Ellipfis may be introduced with Propriety: But if we would be more exprefs and emphatical, it muft not be admitted.

"*My* Lord and *my* God. *My* Sons and *my* Daughters."

"This is the Man they hate. Thefe are the Goods they bought. Are thefe the Gods they worfhip? Is this the Woman you faw?"

In fuch common Forms of Speech the *relative Pronoun* is ufually omitted: Though for the moft Part, efpecially in complex Sentences, it is much better to have it expreffed.

"In the Pofture I lay. In the Way I went. The Horfe I rode fell down."

Better fay, "The Pofture in *which* I lay. The way in *which* I went. The Horfe *on which* I rode fell down."

The Antecedent and the Relative conneƈt the Parts of a Sentence together,

ther, and fhould, to prevent Confufion and Obfcurity, anfwer to each other with great Exactnefs.

"We fpeak *that* we do know, and "teftify *that* we have feen."

The Ellipfis, in fuch Inftances, is manifeftly improper: Let it therefore be fupplied. "We fpeak that *which* "we do know, and teftify that *which* "we have feen."

The Relative, *what*, in the neuter Gender, feems to include both the Antecedent and the Relative. "This is "*what* you fpeak of, i. e. The Thing "*which* you fpeak of."

## The ELLIPSIS *of the* VERB.

" The Man *was* old and crafty, i. e. " The Man *was* old and the Man *was* " crafty."

" She *was* young and rich, and " beautiful. Thou *art* poor, and " wretched, and miferable, and blind, " and naked."

But if we would, in such Enumerations, point out one Property above the rest, let that Property be put last, and the Ellipsis supplied.

"She is young and beautiful, and "*she* is rich."

"I *recommended* the Father and Son: "We *saw* the Town and Country. "He *rewarded* the Women and Children."

"You *ought* to love and serve Him. "I *desire* to hear and learn. He *went* "to see and hear, i. e. He *went* to see, "and *he went* to hear."

In which last Instances, there is not only an Ellipsis of the governing Verb, but likewise of the Sign of the infinitive Mode which is governed by it.

And here it may not be amiss to observe, that some Verbs, through Custom at least, seem to require the Ellipsis of this Sign.

"I *bid*

"I *bid* you rife and go. He *made* me "go and do it. I *heard* him curfe and "fwear. I *faw* her go that Way. You "*need* not fpeak. Would you *have* me "call?"

In all which Inftances the Sign of the infinitive Mode would be improper.

*The* ELLIPSIS *of the Adverb, Prepofition, Conjunction, and Interjection.*

"He fpake and acted *wifely*. They "fing and play *moft delightfully*. She "*foon* found and acknowledged her "Miftake. *Thrice* I went and offered "my Service," that is, "*Thrice* I "went, and *thrice* I offered my Ser-"vice."

"They confefs the Power, Wif-"dom, Goodnefs, *and* Love of their "Creator, i. e. The Power, *and* "Wifdom, *and* Goodnefs, *and* Love."

"May I fpeak of Power, Wifdom, "Goodnefs, Truth?"

The entire Ellipsis of the Conjunction, as in the last Instance, occurs but seldom: In some particular Cases, however, it may have its Propriety.

" Though I love, I do not adore
" him. Though he went up, he could
" see nothing; i. e. Though I love
" Him, *yet* I do not adore Him."

" I desire you would come to me.
" He said he would do it, i. e. He said
" *that* he would do it."

These Conjunctions may be sometimes omitted; but for the most Part, it it much better to express them.

There are several *Parts* of *Correspondent Conjunctions*, or such as answer to each other in the Construction of a Sentence, which should be carefully observed, and perhaps never, suppressed.

*That*, answering to *so*. " It is *so* ob-
" vious *that* I need not mention it."

*As* answering to *so*. "The City of
"*Bristol* is not near *so* large *as* that of
"*London.*"

*So* answering to *as*. "*As* is the
"Priest *so* are the People."

*As* answering to *as*. "She is *as* tall
"*as* you."

*Nor* answering to *neither*. "*Neither*
"the one, *nor* the other."

*Or* answering to *either*. "*Either* this
"Man *or* that Man."

*Or* answering to *whether*. "*Whether*
"it were I *or* you."

*Yet* answering to *though* or *although*.
"*Though* she was young, *yet* she was
"not handsome."

PREPOSITIONS *are often suppressed.*

"He went *into* the Churches, Halls,
"and public Buildings: *Through* the
"Streets and Lanes of the City: He
"spake

" fpake to every Gentleman and Lady
" of the Place; i.e. *To* every Gentle-
" man and *to* every Lady."

" I did him a Kindnefs. He brought
" me the News. She gave him the
" Letters; i. e. She gave *to* him the
" Letters."

The Ellipfis of the Interjection is
not very common.

" *O* Pity and Shame!"
*Milton.*"

EXAMPLES *of the* ELLIPSIS.

" If good Manners will not juftify
" my long Silence, Policy, at leaft,
" will. And you muft confefs, there
" is fome Prudence in not owning a
" Debt one is incapable of paying."

If good Manners will not juftify my
long Silence, Policy at leaft will, *juftify
it:* And you muft confefs, *that*, there is
fome Prudence in not owning a Debt,
*which*, one is incapable of paying.
*Fitzofborn's Letters.*
"He

"He will often argue, that if this Part of our Trade were well cultivated, we should gain from one Nation; and if another, from another."

He will often argue, that if this Part of our Trade were well cultivated, we should gain from one Nation; and if another *Part of our Trade were well cultivated, we should gain*, from another *Nation*.

*Addison's Spect.*

"Could the Painter have made a Picture of me, capable of your Conversation, I should have sat to him with more Delight than ever I did to any Thing in my Life."

Could the Painter have made a Picture of me, *which could have been*, capable of your Conversation, I should have sat to him with more Delight than ever I did, *sit*, to any Thing in my Life."

*Mr. Locke to Mr. Molyneux.*

A few instances in which perhaps all possible elliptical Words are supplied.

"You

"You must renounce the Conversation of your Friends, and every civil Duty of Life, to be concealed in gloomy and unprofitable Solitude."

You must renounce the Conversation of your Friends, and, *you must renounce*, every civil Duty of Life, to be concealed in gloomy, *Solitude, and you must renounce the Conversation of your Friends, and you must renounce every civil Duty of Life, to be concealed in,* unprofitable Solitude.

*Fitzosborn's Letters.*

"When a Man is thoroughly persuaded that he ought neither to admire, wish for, *or* pursue any Thing but what is actually his Duty, it is not in the Power of Seasons, Persons, *or* Accidents, to diminish his Value."

When a Man is thoroughly persuaded that he ought neither to admire, *any Thing but what is actually his Duty to admire, and when a Man is thoroughly persuaded, that he ought neither to* wish for *any Thing but what is actually his Duty*
*to*

*to wish for*, or, *when a Man is thoroughly persuaded that he ought not to* pursue any Thing but what is actually his Duty, *to pursue;* it is not in the Power of Seasons, *to diminish his Value, and it is not in the Power of* Persons, *to diminish his Value,* or, *it is not in the Power of,* Accidents to diminish his Value.

*Addison's Spect.*

The following Instances are produced to shew the Impropriety of Ellipsis, in some particular Cases.

" That learned Gentleman, if he
" had read my Essay quite through,
" would have found several of his Ob-
" jections might have been spared."

It should have been—Would have found, *that,* several of his Objections, &c.

" I scarce know any Part of Natu-
" ral Philosophy would yield more
" Variety and Use."

NOTE. *Or,* which occurs twice in the *elliptical Sentence* above, is rather an Impropriety; it should have been *nor*.

Any

—Any Part of Natural Philosophy, *which* would yield more Variety and Use.

"You and I cannot be of two Opinions; nor, I think, any two Men used to think with Freedom."

— Nor, I think any two Men, *who are* used to think with Freedom.

*Mr. Locke to Mr. Molyneux.*

Some Sentences which seem to differ from the common Forms of Construction accounted for on the Supposition of Ellipsis.

"*By preaching Repentance.* By the preaching of Repentance.

Both these are supposed to be proper and synonimous Expressions, and I cannot but think, the former is an Ellipsis of the latter, in which the Article and the Preposition are both suppressed by Custom.

*By*

# APPENDIX.

*By Preaching of Repentance;* and, *By the Preaching Repentance;* are both judged to be improper. These Sentences are partly elliptical, and partly not so, and from hence the Impropriety seems to arise. *Preaching,* in either Form, is a Substantive distinguished by the Sense, and a Preposition prefixt to it: Nor is the Noun following governed by the supposed verbal Force of the Word, *Preaching,* but by the Preposition expressed or understood.

" *Well is Him. Wo is me. Wo un-*
" *to you.*"

These Sentences are all elliptical, and partly explain each other.

Well is *it for* Him.   Wo is *to* me. Wo *is* unto you.

To have recourse to a supposed *dative* Case is therefore quite unnecessary.

" My Father is greater than I. She
" loves him better than me."

My Father is greater than I *am*. She loves him better than, *she loves*, me.

" To let blood. To let down."

To let, *out*, Blood; or, To let Blood *run out*. To let, *it fall* or *slide*, down.

" To go a Fishing. To go a Hunt-
" ing."

To go a Fishing *Voyage*. To go *on* a Hunting *Party*.

" To walk a Mile. To sleep all
" night."

To walk *through the Space of* a Mile. To sleep *through* all *the* Night.

" A hundred Sheep. A thousand
" Men."

A *Flock of one* Hundred Sheep. A *Company of one* Thousand Men.

" That Man has a Hundred a Year."
That

That Man has *an Income of* a Hundred *Pounds in* a Year.

" A few Men. A great many
" Men."

A *Hundred*, a *Thousand*, *Few*, *Many*, are to be confidered as collective Nouns; and diftinguifhed as fuch by the fingular Article:

A few (i.e. a fmall Number) *of* Men. A great many (i.e. a great Number) *of* Men.

" He is the better for you. The
" deeper the Well, the clearer the
" Water."

An Article feems, for the moft Part, to be the Sign of a Noun either expreffed or underftood; and the above Sentences may be refolved thus:

He is the better *Man* for you. The deeper *Well*, the Well *is*, the clearer *Water*, the Water *is*.

"He descending, the doors being shut."

This is commonly called the Case or State Absolute, and, in English, the Pronoun must be in the *Nominative*. The Sentence seems to be elliptical, and the Meaning is,

*While* he *was* descending, *while* the Doors *were* shut.

"He came into this World of *ours*;

"I am justified in publishing any Letters of Mr. *Locke*'s.

In the first of these Instances the genitive Case of the Pronoun comes after the Preposition, but cannot be governed by it, for then it would be the Accusative: It must therefore be governed by some other Word understood in the Sentence.

He came into this World of our *Dwelling, Habitation,* &c.

And

And then omitting the Noun it will be, This World of *ours*, by the common Rules of Conſtruction.

The other Sentence may be explained after the ſame Manner.

I am juſtified in publiſhing any Letters of Mr. Locke's *Writing, Correſpondence*, &c. i. e. of the Writing or Correſpondence of Mr. Locke.

The Uſe of the genitive Caſe, in ſuch Inſtances, ſeems to be a little uncouth. And here I cannot but obſerve that though, on ſome Occaſions, the Genitive has its Propriety and Elegance, yet it ſhould, in the General, be uſed with Caution, and much more ſparingly, perhaps, than ſome Authors have done.

EXERCISES* of *bad* English, to be corrected for the Improvement of the *young* Scholar.

## EXERCISE I.

I *Hates*, thou *doth* laugh, he *dost* play; we *weepeth*, ye *does* walk, they *doth* read.

I *art* trying, thou *is* idling, he *are* talking; we *art* going, ye *is* seeking, they *am* tarrying.

I *didst* ask, thou *denied*, he *performedst*; we did *demanded*, ye did *sleeps*, they *didst* return.

I *wast* marching, thou *were* writing, he *wast* exercised; we *was* passing, ye *wast* speaking, they *was* running.

* The Learner is desired to take Notice, that such Words, as in these Exercises require Correction, will be found printed in *Italics*.

EXERCISE

# EXERCISE II.

I *Haſt* heard, thou *hath* broken, ye *have* behaved; we *has* belied, ye *hath* ſworn, they *has* counterfeited.

I *hath* been betrayed, thou *has* been deceived, he *have* been tempted; we *has* been compared, ye *hath* been taken, they *haſt* been deſpiſed.

I *hadſt* eſcaped, thou *had* been condemned, he *hadſt* been confounded; we *ſhalt* deliver, ye *ſhalt* have poſſeſſed, they *wilt* ſucceed.

I *mayeſt* continue, thou *will* enlarge, he *mighteſt* have bleſt; we *ſhouldeſt* envy, he *oughteſt* to *hath* finiſhed, they *ſhalt hath* entertained.

# EXERCISE III.

THE Drums *beats*. The Dog *bark*. Birds *flies*. The Child *are* crying. The Parrot *chatter*. Cats *mews*. The Mice *is* playing.

Many

Many days *has* paſt. I *were* very ſorrowful. My father *waſt* angry. Such Perſons *is* much eſteemed. Virtue *gain* Credit.

I and my Siſter *walks* often together. Thou and thy Couſin *is* always wrangling. Honour and Reſpect *waits* on Goodneſs.

This *Fellows wilt* be troubleſome. My Mother loves him better than *I*. John *delivereſt* the Letter to *thou*. That is the Man, *who* thou *ſaw* Yeſterday.

### EXERCISE IV.

THIS Book is *more thicker* than thine. She is the *moſt wiſeſt* of the three. Get me your *Brother* Knife. That *wilt* add to your *Son* Diſgrace. It is a moſt *ſhockingeſt* Thing.

Years *ſlides* faſt away, and old Age *creep* on apace. Uſe *make* Artiſts and inſenſibly *give* Dexterity. Flattery *are* odious, but *have* many *Admirer*. Vices
 *imitates*

## APPENDIX. 137

*imitates* Virtues, and by that Means *deceives* us. Profperity *haft* numerous Followers, but Adverfity *bring* Contempt.

Whilft we *was* hunting, ye *was* ftudying. She *have* always highly valued *thou*, though thou *has* not believed it. They *fays* that the King *am* coming, and that he *wilt* make a grand Appearance.

## EXERCISE V.

A Wife Man *wilt* hear, and will *increafeth* Learning; and a Man of Underftanding *fhalt attains* unto wife Counfels.

My Son *forgets* not my Law, but let thine Heart *keeps* my Commandments.

*Withhold* not Good from *they* to *who* it *art* due, when it *are* in the Power of thine Hand to *does* it.

Hear

Hear, ye *Child*, the Instruction of a Father, and *attendeth* to *knows* Understanding.

*Keepeth* thy *Hearts* with all Diligence, for out of it *is* the Issues of Life.

## EXERCISE VI.

GO to the Ant, thou *Sluggard's*: *considereth* her Ways, and be wise.

*Wisdom are betterer* than Rubbies; and all the *Thing* that *mayest* be desired *is* not to be compared unto it.

*Treasure* of Wisdom profit nothing; but Righteousness *deliverest* from Death.

The merciful Man *do* good to his own Soul; but he, that *are* cruel *trouble* his own Flesh.

*Children* Children *is* the Crown of old men; and the Glory of Children *are* their Fathers.

EXERCISE

## EXERCISE VII.

THE Lord *know* the Way of the Righteous; and the Way of the ungodly *shalt perisheth*.

Let *we* break their Bonds afunder, and *casts* away their cords from us.

My Soul *are* fore troubled; but, Lord, how long *will* thou *punisheth I*?

The wicked *shalt* be *turn* into Hell, and all the People that *forgets* God.

Confider and *heareth* me, O Lord, my God; *lightenest* mine *Eye*, that I *sleeps* not in Death.

## EXERCISE VIII.

GOD *art* bur Hope and Strength; a very prefent *Helps* in Trouble.

No Man *mayest* deliver his Brother; nor *makes* Agreement unto God for *them*.

Verily

Verily there *are* a Reward for the Righteous; doubtless there is a God that *judge* the Earth.

Thou *crowneth* the Year with thy Goodness; and thy Clouds *drops* Fatness.

I *knows*, O Lord, that thy Judgments *is* right; and that thou of very Faithfulness *have cause* me to be troubled.

## EXERCISE IX.

VIRTUE both *give* Quiet of Life, and *takest* away the Terror of Death.

There *art* nothing so easy, but it becomes hard when thou *does* it with an unwilling *Minds*.

Nothing *delight* me so much as the *Work* of God.

To be always happy *are* to be ignorant of one *Parts* of the *Thing* of Nature.

They

# APPENDIX. 141

They *art* free from Fear, *whom has* done nothing amiss; but they, who *haſt* committed Sin, always *thinks* Puniſhment *hover* before *his* Eyes.

Pleaſure and Amuſement, purſued with Moderation, *is* as requiſite for the *Preſervations* of Health, as Heat, Air, and Moiſture, *is* for the Growth of Plants and Flowers.

## EXERCISE X.

KNOWLEDGE, which *are* ſeparated from Juſtice, *art* to be *call* Craft rather than Wiſdom.

The Ignorance of Youth *oughteſt* to be directed by the Experience of old Man.

Whatever thou *ſhall* undertake, always *imagines* that God *ſtand* a *Witneſſes* of the *Actions*.

Let *we* deſpiſe earthly *Thing*, and *thinkeſt* upon *that who* are heavenly and divine.

N        Without

Without Chastity, however fair the *Bodies mayest* be, it cannot *is* amiable.

*Does* not thou *composest* thy Eyes to Sleep, before thou *have* revolved on all the *Action* of the *Days* past.

## EXERCISE XI.

YOUNG *Person* are not less indebted to their Teachers for the good and wise *Instruction* that are given *him*, than they *is* to their Parents *which broughtest* them into Existence.

When the *Amounts* of all earthly Acquirements *art* duly *consider*, it *wilt* be found to be very little, if any *Things*, more than—Vanity and *Vexations*.

We *wert* born for Society and the Community of Mankind, and therefore *shouldest* contribute as much as *are* in our Power to the common *Benefits*.

Bitter Enemies *deserves* much better of us than those pretended *Friend which* would *enticeth* us into Wickedness.

EXERCISE

# EXERCISE XII.

THE due Management of the early Part of Life *are* of such singular Importance to the future Welfare of Men, that *he* are usually good or bad according to the good or bad *Principle* they then *imbibes*.

*Person* of high Spirit strive to conceal *his* Grief and Distress from the World as much as *he* are able; not because they *wishes* to be deemed insensible of Feeling, but because they *wouldest appears* to *suffereth* with Firmness, rather than *becomes* the *Object* of Pity, which, whilst it *mayest brings* Relief, *banish* Admiration.

It *are* one great *Provinces* of Reason to *suppresses* sanguine Expectations from any Thing below; since many unforeseen *Accident* may *overthroweth* in a *Moments* those *Scheme*, which had been *formeth* for Years with Care, Deliberation, and Secresy.

# EXERCISE XIII.

IT *are report* of Hercules, that, when he *grow* up towards Manhood, *they* went into a lonely *Places*, and there *sit* down, deliberated with *herself* a long *Times*, whether he *shouldst gave* himself up to the *Way* of Virtue or Pleasure.

Plato *wroteth* to Archytas, that he *were* born not for himself alone, but likewise for his *Countries* and his *Friend*.

Pythagoras *thoughteth them* to be a Wickedness that Body *shouldst* be *fatten* by *Bodies*, or that *ones* Animal should be *supporteth* by the *Deaths* of another.

When a *Persons* once *offereth* to *teaches* Themistocles the *Arts* of *remembered* all *Thing*, Themistocles *repliest*, that he *woudst does her* a much more acceptable *Favors*, if he would *taught* him how to forget those Things, *who* he wished not to *remembers*.

EXERCISE

# EXERCISE XIV.

ALEXANDER was at length *convince*, how much more *happier* he *were* which *covetedst* Nothing, than he who *require* the Government of the whole *Worlds*.

It *were* a *Sayings* of Demetrius, that no *ones* was a more *unhappier* Person than him, to *who* no Adversity *hadst* ever *happening*.

Notwithstanding Xerxes was *replenisheth* with all the *Blessing* of Body and *Fortunes*, yet, not content therewith, he *proposeth* a Reward to him, *which* should *invents* a new *Kinds* of Pleasure.

The Athenians, though the *wise* and most *learnedest* of all the Greeks, *condemnedst* Socrates to *dies*, because he *teached* the Unity of God, and the Spirituality of the *Worships* that *are* due to him.

Isocrates used to *calls* Boy of a ready Genius the *Son* of the Gods.

# EXERCISE XV.

FOR a confiderable *Times* after the Deluge, Hunting *feem* to *haft be* one of the principal *Employment* of *mankinds*, on account of the great Number of wild *Beaft* with *whom* the World then *abounds*. Nimrod difplaying particular Skill and Activity in this *Exercifes*, *were* *advances* to great Honour, and at length *acquireth* fuch *an* Supremacy over his *Cotemporary*, as to be *enable* to *founds* the *Cities* of Babylon, and *eftablifheth* the firft Monarchy of *who* Hiftory *make* mention.

The Religion of Antiquity, *who prevails* the longeft, and *extendeft* the fartheft, *waft* the *Doctrines* of a Plurality of *God*, and *feem* to *haft* acquired *their* Influence in the rudeft *Age* of Society, while the *Effort* of Reafon *wert* feeble, and Imagination and Paffion *direct* the *Conducts*.

The *Phenician* have been univerfally *allows* by Pagan *Writer* to be the firft People,

People, *which cultivateth* the *Art* subservient to Navigation.

## EXERCISE XVI.

A Taste for what *were* superb and magnificent *seem* to *has* been the *distinguish* Character of the Egyptians, *Babylonian*, and Assyrians, which *he* chiefly *displayeth* in their *Work* of Architecture, though without any Pretension to *Elegances*.

The History of the Roman Emperors *present we* with a Set of *Wretch*, that, if we *excepts* only a few, were an absolute *Disgraces* to human Nature.

The Greeks *wast* the first *Person*, *which hadst* the happy *Arts* of uniting Beauty to Magnificence, and Elegance *of* Grandeur, Composition also, in a great Variety of *Branch, were carry* by *him* to a *Degrees* of Perfection, of which few *Modern* can *forms* a tolerable Idea: whilst Philosophy *were* cultivate-

*tivate* with singular Success. And that *his* active was not inferior to their speculative Talents, *appear* plainly from the several famous Statesmen and *Warrior* which at different *Perioa springs* up amongst them.

## EXERCISE XVII.

IN the *Reigns* of David, the *Descendant* of Aaron had *multiply* to such a Degree, that they *couldst* not all *dia* Duty in the Temple at once; he therefore divided *him* into twenty-four *Course*, and *ordains* that they should *ministered* weekly by *turn*.

So greatly prejudiced *was* the Jews against the Heathens around *him*, that they fancied the very Dust of any of their *Country pollute* them; and therefore *use* to *wipes* their Feet at the Borders of *his* own Land, lest *he* should *defileth* the holy Inheritance.

In many *Part* of the East it *have* long *be* an usual Thing to *has* at Feasts *a* airy
Kinds

*Kinds* of Music *accompany* with Dancing; but at *Funeral*, melancholy Airs, *joins* with the Lamentations of *Person*, chiefly *Woman*, hired for the Purpose.

## EXERCISE XVIII.

ENGLAND, being *wash* by the Sea on three of *it Side*, is exempted from *that* Extremes of *Heats* and Cold, to which other *Country*, lying under the same *Degree* of Latitude, *art expose*; and, on this *Accounts*, is favourable to the Longevity of *their Inhabitant* in general.

China *are* said to be *divide* into fifteen *Province*, each of *whom*, for *their* Extent, Fruitfulness, Riches, and Populousness, might well be *reckon* a *Kingdoms* of *themselves*. The *Account*, however, *who us* yet have of this vast *Empires*, are *suspecting* to *is* far from true.

Galilee *wast* divided into two *Part*, whereof the upper was *calleth* Galilee of the *Gentile*, because *they border* upon on the Gentile Nations, and was in some Measure *inhabits* by them. The whole Country *were* situate to the North of Palestine, and, as Josephus *inform* us, exceedingly populous and fruitful.

## EXERCISE XIX.

THE principal *Cause* of Idolatry amongst the Heathens were four; the first of *whose were*, the excessive Folly and vain Glory of *Man;* the second, the abject Flattery of *Subject* towards *his Prince;* the third, an immoderate *Loves* of Immortality; and the fourth, an extravagant Desire of *perpetuates* the Remembrance of good and excellent *Man*.

As the *Romans* People *was distributeth* into three *Rank*; namely, that of Senators or *Nobleman,* *Knight* or Gentlemen, and *Plebeian* or *Citizen;* so was the Roman Gods also *divides* into three *Class*.

The

The first *Classes* is that of the Superior, Select, or Celestial *God*, and *were* twenty in *Numbers*; twelve whereof *was stile* Consentes, because, in *Matter* of great *Moments*, Jupiter *admittedst him* into *their* Council: the second Class contains such, as were *deify* on account of *his Merit*; the third, those whose *Virtue* rendered *him* somewhat superior to *Mortal*, though not equal to the *others God*.

We shall now add a few *Lessons*, relative to the *English Language*; which may serve at Pleasure, as a farther *Praxis* both on the *Grammatical Institutes*, and the *Strictures* on the *Ellipsis*.

## LESSON I.

GRAMMAR being the Key to all Science, a due Regard has generally been paid to it by Men of the best Sense, and most extensive Knowledge. Among the ancient Romans, Persons of the highest Character for Dignity and Learning, did not think the Cultivation and Improvement of their native Tongue beneath their Attention;

Attention; as we learn from their Writers. Nor have some laudable Attempts of that Kind been wanting, both formerly and of late Years, with Regard to the *English* Language; though much remains yet to be done, for bringing it to a regular and complete System in all its Parts.

Dr. WARD.

## LESSON II.

THE *English* Language hath been much cultivated during the last two hundred Years. It hath been considerably polished and refined; its Bounds have been greatly enlarged; its Energy, Variety, Richness, and Elegance, have been abundantly proved by numberless Trials, in Verse and in Prose, upon all Subjects, and in every Kind of Style: But whatever other Improvements it may have received, it hath made no advances in *grammatical* Accuracy. *Hooker* is one of the earliest Writers of confiderable Note within the Period above-mentioned: Let his Writings be compared with the beft of thofe of more modern Date, and I believe it will be found, that in Correctnefs, Propriety, and Purity of *Englifh* Style, he hath hardly been furpaffed, or even equalled, by any of his Succeffors. It is now above fifty Years fince Dr. *Swift* made a public Remonftrance, addreffed to the Earl of *Oxford*, of the imperfect State of our Language; 'alleging in particular, " That in many In- " ftances it offended againft every Part " of Grammar."—But let us confider, how, and in what Extent, we are to underftand this Charge. — Does it mean, that the Englifh Language, as it is fpoken by the politeft Part of the Nation, and as it ftands in the Writings of our moft approved Au hors, often offends againft every Part of Grammar? Thus far, I am afraid, the Charge is true. Or does it farther imply, that our Language is in its Nature irregular and capricious; not hitherto fubject, nor eafily reducible, to

a Syftem

a System of Rules? In this respect, I am persuaded, the Charge is wholly without Foundation.  Dr. LOWTH.

## LESSON III.

A Gentleman ought to study Grammar among the other Helps of speaking well: I mean the Grammar of his *own Tongue*, of the Language he uses, that he may understand his own Country Speech, and speak it properly, without shocking the Ears of those it is addressed to with Solecisms and offensive Irregularities—And to this Purpose Grammar is necessary. Whether all Gentlemen should not do this, I leave to be considered; since the Want of Propriety and grammatical Exactness is thought very misbecoming in one of that Rank, and usually draws on one guilty of such Faults, the Censure of having had a lower Breeding, and of having mixed with worse Company, than suits with his Situation in Life.

If this be so (as I suppose it is), it will be Matter of Wonder why young Gentlemen

tlemen are never once told of the Grammar of their own Tongue:—Nor is their own Language ever propofed to them as worthy their Care and cultivating, though they have daily Ufe of it, and are often, in their future Courfe of Life, judged of by their handfome or awkward Way of addreffing themfelves in it.

LOCKE on Education.

## LESSON IV.

THE *Englifh* delight in Silence more than any other *European* Nation, if the Remarks which are made on us by Foreigners are true. Our Difcourfe is not kept up in Converfation, but falls into more Paufes and Intervals than in neighbouring Countries; as it is obferved, that the Matter of our Writing is thrown much clofer together, and lies in a narrower Compafs, than is ufual in the Works of foreign Authors.

This Humour fhews itfelf in feveral Remarks that we may make upon the *Englifh Language*. As, firft of all, by its abridgabounding in Monosyllables, which gives us an Opportunity of delivering our Thoughts in few Sounds. This indeed takes off from the Elegance of our Tongue, but at the same Time expresses our Ideas in the readiest Manner, and consequently answers the first Design of Speech, better than the Multitude of Syllables, which make the Words of other Languages more *tunable* and *sonorous*.

In the next Place we may observe, that where the Words are not Monosyllables, we often make them so, as much as lies in our Power, by our Rapidity of Pronunciation; as it generally happens in most of our long Words which are derived from the *Latin*, where we contract the Length of the Syllables that give them a grave and solemn Air in their own Language, to make them more proper for Dispatch, and more conformable to the Genius of our own Tongue.

The same Aversion to Loquacity has of late Years made a very considerable Alteration in our Language, by closing in one Syllable the Termination of

O our

our preterperfect Tense, which has very much disfigured the Tongue, and turned a tenth Part of our smoothest Words into so many Clusters of Consonants. This is the more remarkable, because the Want of Vowels in our Language has been the Complaint of our politest Authors, who neverthelefs are the Men that have made these Retrenchments, and consequently very much increased our former Scarcity.

This Reflection on the Words that end in *ed*, I have heard in Conversation from one of the greatest Geniuses this Age has produced. I think we may add to the foregoing Observation, the Change which has happened in our Language, by the Abbreviation of several Words that are determined in *eth*, by substituting an *s* in the Room of the last Syllable.—This has wonderfully multiplied a Letter, which was before too frequent in the *English* Tongue, and added to that Hissing in our Language, which is taken so much Notice of by Foreigners; but at the same Time humours our Taciturnity, and eases us of many superfluous Syllables.

Addison's Spect.

# LESSON V.

The humble Petition of W HO and
WHICH,

Sheweth,

THAT your Petitioners being in a forlorn and deſtitute Condition, know not to whom we ſhall apply ourſelves for Relief, becauſe there is hardly any Man alive who hath not injured us. Nay, we ſpeak it with Sorrow, even *you* yourſelf, whom we ſhould ſuſpect of ſuch a Practice the leaſt of all Mankind, can hardly acquit yourſelf of having given us ſome Cauſe of Complaint. We are deſcended of ancient Families, and kept up our Dignity and Honour many Years, till the Jackſprat T H A T ſupplanted us. How often have we found ourſelves ſlighted by the Clergy in their Pulpits, and the Lawyers at the Bar! Nay, how often have we heard in one of the moſt polite and auguſt Aſſemblies in the Univerſe, to our great Mortification, theſe Words, *That* THAT *that noble Lord urged!* which, if one of us had had Juſtice done, would have ſounded no-
bler

bler thus: *That* WHICH *that noble Lord urged.* Senators themselves, the Guardians of British Liberty, have degraded us, and preferred THAT to us; and yet no Decree was ever given against us. In the very Acts of Parliament, in which the utmost Right should be done to every *Body*, *Word*, and *Thing*, we find ourselves often either not used, or used one instead of another. In the first and best Prayer Children are taught, they learn to misuse us: *Our Father* WHICH *art in Heaven*, should be *Our Father* WHO *art in Heaven;* and even a CONVOCATION, after long Debates, refused to consent to an Alteration. The *Spanish* Proverb says, *A wise Man changes his Mind, a Fool never will.* So that we think *you*, Sir, a very proper Person to address to, since we know you to be capable of being convinced, and changing your Judgment. You are well able to settle this Affair, and to you we submit our Cause. We desire you to assign the Butts and Bounds of each of us: And that for the future we may both enjoy our own.

    And your Petitioners, &c.
      SPECT. *R.*

## LESSON VI.

The just Remonstrance of affronted
THAT.

THOUGH I deny not the Petition of Mess. *Who* and *Which*, yet you should not suffer them to be rude, and to call honest People Names; for that bears very hard on some of those Rules of Decency which you are justly famous for establishing. They may find Fault, and correct Speeches in the Senate and at the Bar: But let them try to get *themselves so often*, and with so much Eloquence, repeated in a Sentence, as a great Orator doth frequently introduce me. "My Lords, says he, with humble Submission, *That that* I say is this: *That that that that* Gentleman has offered, is not *that that* he should have proved to your Lordships. Let those two questionary Petitioners try to do this with their *Whos* and their *Whiches*."—[Besides] How can a judicious Man distinguish one Thing from another without saying, *This here*, or, *That there*? And how can a sober Man,

with-

without using the Expletives of Oaths (in which indeed the Rakes and Bullies have a great Advantage over others) make a Discourse of any tolerable Length without *That is;* and, if he be a very grave Man indeed, without *That is to say?* And how instructive as well as entertaining are those usual expressions, in the Mouths of great Men, *Such Things as That*, and *the like of That!*

I am not against reforming the Corruptions of Speech you mention, and own there are proper Seasons for the Introduction of other Words besides *That*; but I scorn as much to supply the Place of a *Who* or a *Which* at every Turn, as they are unequal always to fill mine; and I expect good Language and civil treatment, and hope to receive it for the future; *That, that* I shall only add, is, *That* I am,

Yours, THAT

SPECTATOR, R.

THE

*Following* Lessons are annexed,

As having a *direct* Tendency to instil

Sentiments of Virtue into Youth.

## LESSON I.

THE ADVANTAGES OF READING AND WRITING.

THE Knowledge of Letters is one of the greatest Blessings that ever God bestowed upon Man. By this Means we preserve for our own Use, through all our Lives, what our Memory would have lost in a few Days, and lay up a rich Treasure of Knowledge for those that shall come after us. By the Art of Reading and Writing, we can sit at Home and acquaint ourselves

selves of what is done in all the diſtant Parts of the World, and find what our Fathers did long ago in the firſt Ages of Mankind. By this Means, a *Briton* holds Correſpondence with his Friend in *America* or *Japan*, and manages all his traffic. We learn by this Means, how the old *Romans* lived, how the *Jews* worſhipped. We learn what *Moſes* wrote, what *Enoch* propheſied, where *Adam* dwelt, and what he did ſoon after the Creation; and thoſe, who ſhall live when the Day of Judgment comes, may learn, by the ſame Means, what we now ſpeak, and what we do in *Great Britain*, or in the Land of *China*.

In ſhort, the Art of Letters does, as it were, revive all the paſt Ages of Men, and ſet them at once upon the Stage; and brings all the Nations from afar, and gives them, as it were, a general Interview: So that the moſt diſtant Nations, and diſtant Ages of Mankind, may converſe together, and grow into Acquaintance.

But the greateſt Bleſſing of all is, the Knowledge of the Holy Scriptures, wherein

wherein God appointed his Servants, in ancient Times, to write down the Discourses which he has made of his Power and Justice, his Providence and his Grace; that we, who live near the End of Time, may learn the Way to Heaven, and everlasting Happiness.

Thus, Letters give us a Sort of Immortality in this World, and they are given us in the Word of God, to support our immortal Hope in the next.

## LESSON II.
### SOLID GLORY AND REAL GREATNESS.

WHATEVER is external to a Man, whatever may be common to good and bad, does not make him truly estimable: we must judge of Men from the Heart; from thence proceed great Designs, great Actions, great Virtues. Solid Glory, which cannot be imitated by Pride, nor equalled by Pomp, resides in personal Qualifications and noble Sentiments. To be good, liberal, beneficent, and generous; to value Riches only for the Sake of diſtributing them; Places of Honour, for the Service of our Country; Power and Credit, to be in a condition to ſuppreſs Vice and reward Virtue; to be really good without ſeeking to appear ſo; to bear Poverty nobly, to ſuffer Injuries and Affronts with Patience, to ſtifle Reſentment, and to do every good Office to an Enemy, when we have it in our Power to be revenged of him; to prefer the public Good to every Thing; to ſacrifice our Wealth, Repoſe, Life, and Fame, if neceſſary, to it: Theſe make a Man truly great and eſtimable.

Take away Probity from the moſt ſhining Actions, the moſt valuable Qualities, and what are they but Objects of Contempt? Are the Drunkenneſs of Alexander, the Murder of his beſt Friends, his inſatiable Thirſt of Praiſe and Flattery, and his Vanity in deſiring to paſs for the Son of Jupiter, though he did not believe it himſelf; are theſe conſiſtent with the Character of a great Prince? When we ſee Marius, and after him Sylla, ſhedding Torrents of Roman Blood for the

Eſtabliſh-

Establishment of their own Power, what Regard can we pay to their Victories and Triumphs?

*Rollin's Method of Study.*

## LESSON III.

### TRUE POLITENESS.

'TIS an Evenness of Soul that excludes at the same Time Insensibility, and too much Earnestness—it supposes a quick Discernment of the different Characters, Tempers, Miseries, or Perfections of Man, and by a sweet Condescension adapts itself to each Man's Case; never to flatter, but always to calm the Passions.—'Tis a Kind of forgetting one's self, in order to be agreeable to others, yet in so delicate a Manner as scarcely to let them perceive you are so employed—it knows how to contradict with Respect, and to please without Sneaking or Adulation; and is equally remote from an insipid Complaisance and a low Familiarity.

*Ramsay's Cyrus.*

## LESSON IV.

### PRUDENCE.

PRUDENCE consists in judging well, what is to be said, and what is to be done, on every new Occasion; when to lie still, and when to be active; when to keep Silence, and when to speak; what to avoid, and what to pursue; how to act in every Difficulty; what Means to make use of to compass such an End; how to behave in every Circumstance of Life, and in all Companies; how to gain the Favour of Mankind, in order to promote our own Happiness, and to do the most Service to God, and the most Good to Men, according to that Station we possess, and those Opportunities we enjoy.

Dr. WATTS on Education.

## LESSON V.

### JUSTICE.

JUSTICE consists in an exact and scrupulous Regard to the Rights of others,

others, with a deliberate Purpose to preserve them on all Occasions sacred and inviolate:—And from this fair and equitable Temper, performing every necessary Act of Justice that relates to their Persons or Properties; being just to their Merits and just to their very Infirmities, by making all the Allowance in their Favour which their Circumstances require, and a good-natured and equitable Construction of particular Cases will admit of; being true to our Friendships, to our Promises, and Contracts; just in our Traffic, just in our Demands, and just by observing a due Moderation and Proportion even in our Resentments.

Discourses on Social Virtue.

## LESSON VI.

### TEMPERANCE.

TEMPERANCE consists in guarding against such an Use of Meats and Drinks, as indisposes the Body for the Service of the Soul, or robs me of my Time—or occasions an Expence beyond what my Circumstances admit —or beyond what will consist with those liberalities to the Poor, which my Relation to God and to them requires—and strongly guarded against whatever has a Tendency to increase a sensual Disposition, or alienate my Soul from Converse with God, and diminish its Zeal and Activity in his Service, or waste my benevolent Temper to Mankind. Dr. DODDRIDGE.

## LESSON VII.

### FORTITUDE.

CHRISTIAN Fortitude, or Courage, is a just Firmness of Soul in the Prospect of Danger in the Way of Duty. It enables us to persevere with Steadiness in the View of the greatest Discouragements and fiercest Opposition.

ACTIVE FORTITUDE is such a Temper of Soul, as enables us to attempt and venture upon any bold Act of Duty, which may endanger our present Ease and worldly Interest, and prompts us to pursue it with a becoming Stea--
dinefs

dineſs and Bravery of Mind, undaunted at every Oppoſition we meet with, and unterrified at all the threatening Dangers that ſtand in our Way.

PASSIVE FORTITUDE is ſuch an habitual Firmneſs and Conſtancy of Soul, as enables us to bear what Sufferings we fall under, without Repining and inward Vexation, and without any outward Tokens of Sinking or Deſpondency; when we ſuſtain heavy Sorrows or Anguiſh of the Fleſh, without any wild or unreaſonable Groanings of Nature, without Rage and unbecoming Reſentment, without Tumult and Confuſion of Spirit; and this ſhould be the Temper of our Souls and Chriſtian Conduct, whether the Sufferings which we feel ariſe from the immediate Hand of God, or from the Injuries and Violence of Men.

Dr. WATTS.

## LESSON VIII.

### THE ORNAMENTS OF YOUTH.

AMONG all the Accompliſhments of Youth, there is none preferable to to a decent and agreeable Behaviour among Men, a modest Freedom of Speech, a soft and elegant Manner of Address, a graceful and lovely Deportment, a cheerful Gravity and good Humour, with a Mind appearing ever serene under the ruffling Accidents of human Life: Add to this, a pleasing Solemnity and Reverence when the Discourse turns upon any Thing sacred and divine, a becoming Neglect of Injuries, a Hatred of Calumny and Slander, a Habit of speaking well of Others, a pleasing Benevolence and Readiness to do Good to Mankind, and special Compassion to the Miserable; with an Air and Conntenance, in a natural and unaffected Manner, expressive of all these excellent Qualifications.

Dr. WATTS on Education.

## LESSON IX.

THE HAPPIEST YOUTH, MANHOOD, AND OLD AGE.

HE, who in his Youth improves his intellectual Powers in the Search of of truth and useful Knowledge, and refines and strengthens his moral and active Powers, by the Love of Virtue, for the Service of his Friends, his Country, and Mankind; who is animated by true Glory, exalted by sacred Friendship for social, and softened by virtuous Love for domestic, Life; who lays his Heart open to every other mild and generous Affection; and who to all these adds a sober masculine Piety, equally remote from Superstition and Enthusiasm: that Man enjoys the most agreeable Youth, and lays in the richest Fund for the honourable Action, and happy Enjoyment, of the succeeding Periods of Life.

He, who in Manhood keeps the defensive and private Passions under the wisest Restraint; who forms the most select and virtuous Friendships; who seeks after Fame, Wealth, and Power, in the Road of Truth and Virtue, and, if he cannot find them in that Road, generously despises them; who, in his private Character and Connexions, gives full Scope to the tender and manly Passions, and in his public Character and Connexion serves his Country

try and Mankind in the moſt upright and diſintereſted Manner; who, in fine, enjoys the Goods of Life with the greateſt Moderation bears its Ills with the greateſt Fortitude; and, in thoſe various Circumſtances of Duty and Trial, maintains and expreſſes an habitual Reverence and Love of God: that Man is the worthieſt Character in this Stage of Life; paſſes through it with the higheſt Satisfaction and Dignity; and paves the Way to the moſt eaſy and honourable Old Age.

Finally, He who, in the Decline of Life, preſerves himſelf moſt exempt from the Chagrins incident to that Period; cheriſhes the moſt equal and kind Affections; uſes his Experience, Wiſdom, and Authority, in the moſt fatherly and venerable Manner; acts under a Senſe of the Inſpection, and with a View to the Approbation, of his Maker; is daily aſpiring after Immortality, and ripening apace for it; and having ſuſtained his Part with Integrity and Conſiſtency to the laſt, quits the Stage with a modeſt and graceful Triumph: this is the beſt, that is the happieſt, Old Man.

# A LIBRARY*
## FOR
### YOUNG GENTLEMEN and LADIES.

*Of the Englifh Language, &c.*

A S H's Grammatical Inftitutes, or An Eafy Introduction to Dr. Lowth's Grammar.
Dr. Lowth's Englifh Grammar.
Fell's Effay toward an Englifh Grammar.
Entick's Child's beft Inftructor in Spelling and Reading.
Entick's New Spelling Dictionary.
Entick's New Latin and Englifh Dictionary.
Knox on a Liberal Education.

* This Library is intended to direct fome tender and valuable Parents, who may poffibly be at a Lofs what Books to buy for their Children; and likewife to gratify fome young People of an inquifitive and ingenious Difpofition, who have a keen Tafte for Books, but for Want of Experience often purchafe Trafh, which not only occafions a Lofs of Time and Money, but is a fad Interruption to real Knowledge, and a wretched Perverfion of the Underftanding and the Heart; and lays a Foundation for fhameful Extravagance and Folly in future Life.

This little Collection, printed in order to fhorten the Path to Knowledge, will doubtlefs be found defective in many Articles. But the Editor was willing to recommend only thofe of which he had certain Knowledge. Every Perfon of good fenfe has it in his Power to add to the Number, with refpect to his own Children.

Dr.

*A* LIBRARY *for*

Dr. Watts's Art of Reading.
Dr. Nugent's New Pocket Dictionary, French and English.
*On Amusements, Lives, &c.*
Mr. Newbery's Books, viz. Mosaic Creation.—New History, of England, 12 mo.—Philosophy for Children.—Circle of the Sciences, 7 Vols.—Atlas Minimus.—Philosophy of Tops and Balls.—Robinson Crusoe.
Beauties of History, or Pictures of Virtue and Vice, drawn from real Life, 2 Vols.
Dodsley's Fables, 12mo.
Gay's Fables, 12mo.
Spectator—Tatler—and Guardian.
Rambler, 4 Vols.—Idler, 2 Vols.
Adventurer, 4 Vols. Connoisseur, 4 Vols.
Tour through Great Britain, 4 Vols.
Plutarch's Lives, translated from the Greek by the Langhornes, 6 Vols.
Knox's Essays, Moral and Literary, 2 Vols.
British Plutarch, containing the Lives of Illustrious Persons, from Hen. VIII. to Geo. II. in 6 Vols. 12mo.
The Moral Miscellany.
The Poetical Miscellany.
Moral and Entertaining Dialogues in English and French, 2 Vols. by Mrs. Vaucluse.

*On Geography.*
Guthrie's Geographical Grammar.
Turner's View of the Earth and Heavens.

### Young Gentlemen *and* Ladies.

Dr. Watts's and Dr. Jennings's Ufe of the Globes.
*Ancient and Modern Hiftory.*
Lockman's Hiftory of England, by Queftion and Anfwer.
Lockman's Roman Hiftory, by Queftion and Anfwer.
Dodfley's Hiftory and Geography of England.
Newbery's Hiftory of the World, 4 Vols.
Boffuet's Univerfal Hiftory, 2 Vols.
Rollin's Ancient Hiftory, 12 Vols.
Hiftory of England in a Series of Letters, 2 Vols.
Belfour's New Hiftory of Scotland.
*Of Arithmetic, &c.*
Walkingame's Arithmetic.
Bonnycaftle's ditto.
Dilworth's Schoolmafter's Affiftant.
Addington's New Syftem of Arithmetic.
Le Clerc's Geometry.
Clare's Youth's Introduction to Trade and Bufinefs.
Mair's Book-keeping. Dilworth's ditto.
*Eloquence and Poetry*
The Poetical Works of Dr. Watts, Milton, Young, Pope, and Gray.
Cotton's Vifions, in Verfe.
Burgh's Art of Speaking.
Enfield's Speaker.
Elegant Extracts.

Q

*A* Library *for*

Historical and Classical Dictionary, 2 Vols.
Cambray's Dialogues on Eloquence.
Rollin's Introduction to the Belles Lettres, or Polite Learning, 4 Vols.
Dr. Akenside on the Pleasures of Imagination.
Dodsley's Collection of Poems, 6 Vols.
Thomson's Seasons.
Gay's Fables.

*Divinity and Morality.*

Watts's Catechisms, complete.
Kenn on the Church Catechism.
The Friendly Instructor, or Familiar Dialogues for the Use of Children.
Derham's Physico and Astro-Theology.
Dr. Young's Night-Thoughts.
Ray's Wisdom of God in the Creation.
Ray's Physico-Theology.
Bunyan's Pilgrim's Progress, two Parts.
Family Instructor, 2 Vols.
Religious Courtship
Dr. Blair's Sermons, 3 Vols.
Fordyce's Sermons to Young Women.
Fordyce's Addresses to Young Men.
Hervey's Meditations, 2 Vols. and on the Education of Daughters.
The Young Misses Magazine, 2 Vols.
The Young Ladies Magazine, 2 Vols.
Instructions for Young Ladies entering the Marriage State, 2 Vols. By M. Beaumont.

Young Gentlemen *and* Ladies.

Murry's Sacred History, with Maps adapted to the Work, 2 Vols. 12mo. 8s.
Scougal's Life of God in the Soul of Man.

*On Education and Science.*

Knox on a liberal Education, 2 Vol.
Knox's Winter Evenings, 3 Vols.
Fordyce's Dialogues on Eudcation, 2 Vols. 8vo.
Ash's Sentiments on Education, 2 Vols.
Watts's Treatise on Education. Locke on Education. Locke's Elements of Natural Philosophy, with the Books on Reading and Study. Locke's Conduct of the Understanding.
Beauties of Natural History.
Description of three Hundred Animals.
Lee's Introduction to Botany.
Martin's Philosophy, 3 Vols.
Spectacle de la Nature, 7 Vols.
Brooke's Natural History of Fossils, Plants, and Animals, 6 Vols.
Spence's Dialogues on Pope's Translation of the Odyssey.
Ferguson's Easy Introduction to Sir Isaac Newton's Philosophy.
Turner's Introduction to Geography.
Watts's Logic and Improvement of the Mind.
Watts's Philosophical Essays.

*A* LIBRARY *for* Young Gentlemen, &c.

*On Letter-Writing, &c.*

Elegant Epistles; or, a Copious Collection of familiar and amusing Letters, large 8vo.

Newbery's Letters on the most common and important Occasions of Life.

Richardson's Collection of Letters. Halifax's Familiar Letters. Fitz-Osborne's Letters. Melmoth's Translation of Pliny's Letter.

Melmoth's Letters of Cicero, translated into English.

*Morals and Maxims of Prudence.*

Tully's Offices, by Cockman.

Œconomy of Human Life.

Fordyce's Elements of Moral Philosophy.

Telemachus, French and English, by Cambray.

Mason's Christian Morals, 2 Vols.

Mason on Self Knowledge.

Dr. Gregory's Advice to his Daughters.

Murray's Mentoria: or, The Young Ladies Instructor.

Mrs. Chapone's Letters on the Improvement of the Mind.

Mrs. Chapone's Miscellanies in Prose and Verse:

Advice from a Lady of Quality to her Children, 2 Vols. By Dr. Glasse.

Percival's Father's Instructions to his Children.

Christian Prudence

F I N I S.

www.ingramcontent.com/pod-product-compliance
Lightning Source LLC
Chambersburg PA
CBHW020253170426
43202CB00008B/354